# Privatization
# of Facility Management
# in Public Hospitals

# Privatization
# of Facility Management
# in Public Hospitals

A Malaysian Perspective

## Hong Poh Fan

PARTRIDGE

ISBN:        Hardcover        978-1-4828-6397-0
             Softcover        978-1-4828-6398-7
             eBook            978-1-4828-6396-3

Print information available on the last page.

**To order additional copies of this book, contact**
Toll Free 800 101 2657 (Singapore)
Toll Free 1 800 81 7340 (Malaysia)
orders.singapore@partridgepublishing.com

www.partridgepublishing.com/singapore

# Contents

# List of Figures

# List of Tables

# Preface

This book is intended for readers who are seeking information about and knowledge of facility management and support services in healthcare facilities like hospitals. It is written to enlighten the reader about the detailed organization processes and workings of a hospital, particularly in the developing country of Malaysia, as the environment and operations of Malaysian hospitals are much different from those in the developed nations of the West. The privatization process that was promulgated was supposed to address the shortcomings that the hospital systems faced within Malaysia at the time of implementation.

A brief history of the privatization development, the concession agreement development, the rationale of the privatization, and the objectives is discussed in Chapter 1.

In Chapter 2, the essence of the concession agreement will be looked into. Not every item will be covered, but the more important ones will be discussed, including the technical requirements and performance indicators (TRPI), master agreed procedures (MAP), hospital-specific implementation plan (HSIP), deduction formula, third-party clauses, centralized management information system (CMIS), quality assurance programme (QAP), reimbursable works. These are important aspects which made the concession agreement unique, with the various parties able to effectively administer the contract.

Chapter 3 is about the five hospital support services (HSS) operated by three concession companies under the purview of the concession agreement (CA). The five HSS are facility engineering maintenance services (FEMS), biomedical engineering maintenance services, cleansing services (CLS), laundry and linen services (LLS), and clinical waste management services (CWMS). The chapter will explain in detail the type of services provided by each of these.

Chapter 4 discusses the monitoring consultant *Sistem Hospital Awasan Taraf* (SIHAT), appointed by the client, Ministry of Health (MOH), Malaysia, to independently administer the CA on behalf of MOH. The consultant's scope of service is discussed in detail in this chapter. The consultant's organizational structure is also detailed within the chapter. Some discussions of reimbursable services and training are included.

Chapter 5 discusses the management information system that was applied in the execution and monitoring of the processes and that was used by the concession companies under the CA. The chapter covers the features and items of the management information system. A listing of the type of reports is provided.

The final chapter, Chapter 6, discusses the benefits and obstacles experienced in the execution of the CA. Concluding remarks are provided. An appendix of the TRPI listings of the five HSS is included for the benefit of the reader. It is hoped that readers will apply some of this information to the context of their working situation and the environment within their own organization or country, as the lessons learnt from this project have led to significant upgrades in the healthcare services of Malaysia.

# Chapter 1

# The Project

## 1.1. Brief History

Facilities management for many organizations and most facilities managers has always been challenging and made up of unrewarding tasks. It is even more challenging and unrewarding if it is for a hospital or a group of hospitals the assets and systems of which are far more complex than those of any commercial or office buildings. This was the situation confronting the Malaysian government in the early 1990s, when many hospitals were operating at a level of service and with standards that were unacceptable to the public. There was no consistency in the healthcare service. The main consequence was the compromise of public healthcare. This impeded growth and progress for public healthcare services in Malaysia.

In 1996, the government of Malaysia took the drastic step of privatizing five core hospital support services nationwide, which was unique, having no parallel elsewhere in the world. The Malaysian government's prime intentions and objectives were to improve healthcare for its population. To facilitate the privatization, a concession agreement between the government of Malaysia and three private companies was signed on 28 October 1996. This privatized hospital support services (HSS) in Malaysia.

Prior to the privatization, all HSS were undertaken by individual hospitals, with no clear coordination between them. It was recognized that HSS was an important component of facilities management in hospitals, without which no hospital could function well. These had to be operated efficiently and be well supported by the management of the hospital, both financially and operationally.

Many of the HSS were either duplicated or lacking at each hospital. This caused the services provided by each hospital to be strained and inefficient. There was no marked improvement to the services provided by the hospital, and each hospital faced problems in providing proper healthcare services on account of this poor coordination and inefficiency. In view of this, the government decided that better services could be provided if common HSS were combined by centralized entities that could spearhead the development of HSS in a coordinated manner, which would lead to better healthcare services provided to the population.

It was decided prior to the signing of the concession agreement in 1996 that five hospital support services, excluding clinical services, be combined and coordinated. These were facility engineering maintenance services (FEMS), biomedical engineering maintenance services (BEMS), cleansing services (CLS), laundry linen services (LLS), and clinical waste management services (CWMS). Three companies were awarded the concession agreement contract for a period of fifteen years, which ended on 27 October 2011. After the period, these companies were in negotiation for a new contract term for the next ten years of service. The companies that were awarded this HSS contract were Faber-Medi-Serve Sdn Bhd, Radicare (M) Sdn Bhd, and Tongkah Medivest Sdn Bhd. Tongkah Medivest Sdn Bhd was later taken over by Pantai Medivest Sdn Bhd.

Following is the geographical area covered by these companies:

- Faber-Medi-Serve Sdn Bhd – The northern zones of Malaysia, including Perak, Kedah, Penang, Perlis, Sabah, and Sarawak
- Radicare (M) Sdn Bhd – Central zone of Kuala Lumpur and Selangor, and eastern zone of Pahang, Terengganu, and Kelantan
- Pantai Medivest Sdn Bhd – Southern zone of Johor, Melaka, and Negeri Sembilan.

In the concession agreement (CA), a total number of 127 hospitals and medical institutions were initially included in the contract. This was expended to 148 hospitals and healthcare institutions at the end of the period.

The initial phase of the concession agreement was disorderly. There were requirements to transfer services, such as laundry and linen and cleaning, which normally had been undertaken by the hospitals themselves, to the new concession companies. Hospital personnel involved in the services were also to be transferred to the companies under new terms of employment. The concession companies (CCs) were required to install centralized plants for laundry linen services and clinical waste incineration. They were given a grace period in order to set up. As the service expanded, the concession companies recruited more staff and workers, who had little or no prior or experience with hospital support services. The centralized management information system (CMIS) had yet to be set up. Thus, there were numerous shortcomings to the services at the commencement of the project.

In addition to the concession agreement with the hospitals, a monitoring consultant was engaged to monitor, evaluate, and inspect the services provided by the concession companies. This monitoring consultant acted as the middleman between the concession companies and the government under the Supervision Unit of the Engineering Service Division of the Ministry of Health, Malaysia. This monitoring consultant, under the name of *Sistem Hospital Awasan Taraf Sdn Bhd*, or SIHAT for short, took an active role in the monitoring the services provided by the contractor throughout the period of the concession agreement.

Included in the contract agreement were the following things:

- Establishment of the technical requirements and performance indicators (TRPI) for each service
- Establishment of master agreed procedures (MAP) for each service
- Establishment of centralized laundry plants and clinical waste incineration plants outside the hospitals
- Use of a deduction formula for non-performance
- Rights of owner to use third-party clauses
- Implementation and maintenance of ISO 9000
- Establishment of a quality assurance programme
- Establishment of a hospital-specific implementation plan (HSIP)
- Training programmes for the hospital
- Establishment of a centralized management information system (CMIS) to monitor the contract
- Provision of technical advice for assets that need upgrading or replacement under reimbursable works.

Besides the above, project operational guidelines (POG) for the five services were established to guide the owners, CCs, hospitals, and consultants on the day-to-day operations. These were drafted by the monitoring consultant and discussed with the Ministry of Health (MOH) and the CCs for effective implementation. During the course of the contract, the contractor made proposals for the hospital engineering planned preventive maintenance (HEPPM) scheme to establish the protocol and checklists for the monitoring of fixed assets and biomedical assets in the hospitals.

The contract was a lump-sum contract for FEMS, BEMS, and CLS on an annual basis, whilst for LLS and CWMS the fee was based on the weights in kilograms of soiled linen and waste respectively.

## 1.2. Rationale of the Privatization

The reasons for the privatization of the hospital support services in the public hospitals were as follows:

- Inefficient equipment and facilities maintenance
- Inconsistency in hospital support services
- Inadequate budget allocation
- Old and obsolete plants and equipment
- High risk of infection from linens and cleansing
- Involvement of clinical staff
- Improper disposal of clinical waste

### 1.2.1. Inefficient Equipment and Facilities Maintenance

Prior to the privatization, planned preventive maintenance (PPM) was not carried out for plants or equipment in the hospitals. This led to frequent breakdowns of the plants and equipment. Repairs were carried out on a reactionary and firefighting basis. Response times to breakdowns were slow, which affected the hospitals' clinical services. Documentation of the life history of equipment was not carried out to monitor the equipment's efficacy. Skilled engineers and technicians were inadequately recruited to operate in all the hospitals. Biomedical equipment was left idle because it was not maintained, as the maintenance staff were unskilled.

## 1.2.2. Inconsistency

Before the privatization, there was no standardization of the support services provided by the hospitals. No definite standards or guidelines were in place. Thus, duplications and substandard procedures and practices were the order of the day. One might have found that the level of services in urban hospitals was better than that of hospitals at the district level, which in the majority serve the rural population. Infection control was compromised at the lower-standard hospitals.

## 1.2.3. Inadequate Budget Allocation

Because of the way hospitals are distributed in the country, there was an inadequately allocated maintenance budget, which led to poor services in the hospitals. Breakdowns were not attended to because the money was not available for repair works or for the purchase of spare parts. At stake was infection control.

## 1.2.4. Old and Obsolete Plants and Equipment in Use

Many old and obsolete plants and equipment were in use, as no comprehensive assets register existed. So that the old and obsolete plants and equipment could be replaced, the implementation of a replacement programme was urgently needed so as not to disrupt the clinical services of the hospitals. Such a program could only be implemented by a central body specifically appointed to study the situation and recommend a replacement. The company appointed to this task needed to have the necessary expertise, knowledge, and experience to undertake the asset-replacement tasks.

## 1.2.5. High Risk of Infection from Linen and Cleansing

Practices and procedures for the usage, distribution, and washing of hospital linens have to be of a high standard to ensure that the risk of infection is minimized. Thus, the consistency of standards is compromised if each hospital has its own practice. This is equally applicable to cleaning practices within the hospitals. Accessories used to clean hospitals need to be consistent, and high standards for cleaning practices must be instituted.

## 1.2.6. Involvement of Clinical Staff

Many complaints had been received from the clinical staff, including the nurses and their auxiliaries, such as sisters and matrons, that their main clinical and nursing duties were compromised because they were also performing non-clinical duties. This could be prevented if specialized workers were employed to perform non-clinical duties like linen distribution or cleaning.

## 1.2.7. Improper Disposal of Clinical Waste

In most of the hospitals, the disposal of clinical waste before the privatization was not well organized. Some had their own incinerators, whereas others had to send their clinical waste to outside facilities or to the nearest hospital that had the required facilities. Many did not meet the Department of Environment standards of environmental disposal. Standards in the transport of clinical waste were badly practised, leaving much room for concern on the control of infection in hospitals. Untimely and poor coordination of clinical waste incineration led to backlogs and posed the hazard of disease outbreaks.

## 1.3. Objectives of the Project

The following were the objectives of the project:

- To ensure that equipment, plants, and facilities were functioning at all times
- To maintain a clean and hygienic hospital environment
- To ensure the proper disposal of clinical waste
- To ensure clean linen supply

## 1.4. Project Overview

The project overview is shown in Figure 1, below, to illustrate the linkages, roles, and responsibilities of the contracting parties in the privatization scheme.

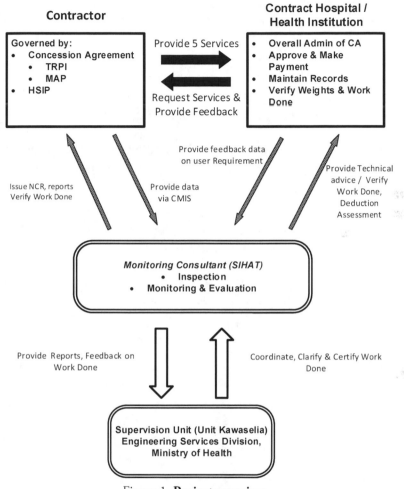

Figure 1 **Project overview**

The contract between the contracting party and the government was called the Concession Agreement (CA). As stated earlier, the contracting party, hereafter called the contractor, consisted of three companies, namely Faber-Medi-Serve Sdn Bhd, Radicare Sdn Bhd, and Tongkah Medivest Sdn Bhd. Another reference to the contractor which is to be used throughout this book is "Concession Company," or CC for short. At the implementation phase, the CCs would have direct dealings with the contract hospitals and health institutions. The CCs' performance and duties were governed by technical requirements and performance indicators (TRPI), the master agreed procedures (MAPS), and the hospital-specific implementation plan (HSIP), as stipulated in the CA. The CCs were to provide five hospital support services, namely FEMS, BEMS,

CLS, LLS, and CWMS, to the hospitals, whilst the hospitals would make a request for the services to the CCs.

The contract hospitals' and health institutions' role was to be the overall administrator of the CA, responsible to approve and make payments, maintain records, and verify weight measurements and work done. They provided feedback to the CCs regarding work performance.

The monitoring consultant SIHAT was employed by the government of Malaysia separately to inspect, monitor, and evaluate the CA. SIHAT's key role was to provide technical advice, verify works done, and recommend deductions during validation meetings. SIHAT also provided feedback data on user requirements to the contract hospitals and issued non-performance reports (NCR) to the CCs, and contractors' performance reports to the MOH.

A fourth party to the contract was the Supervision Unit (in Malay, the Unit *Kawaselia*) of the Engineering Services Division of MOH, which, although not in direct contact with the CCs, played an important role in addressing key issues of the CA. The unit coordinated, clarified, and certified works carried out by the CCs.

# Chapter 2

# Essence of the Concession Agreement

## 2.1. Introduction

There are many aspects of the concession agreement (CA), which is unique and differs from the norm. This chapter will highlight those key components for the interest of the reader. The key components are as follows:

- Technical requirements and performance indicators (TRPI)
- Master agreed procedures (MAP)
- Hospital-specific implementation plan (HSIP)
- Deduction formula
- Third-party clauses
- Centralized management information system (CMIS)
- Quality assurance programme (QAP)
- Reimbursable works

## 2.2. Hierarchy of Contract Management

Figure 2  **Hierarchy of HSS Contract Management**

In the management of the concession agreement, the process and approaches commenced as from the concession agreement contract (CAC) which highlighted the roles and responsibilities of all parties to the contract. Thus, this established the CA at the pinnacle of the administrative process and management. Within the CA, obligations, roles, responsibilities and procedures were scripted out in the TRPI and MAP.

HSIP was not part of the CA but constituted an important component of the management process as the document provided specific information and procedures in each contract hospital. To support the HSIP and administration of CA, it was necessary to record and report all activities not only for payment but also to monitor all progress and processes which could be useful to improve the hospital support service (HSS) in the future. Records and reports were important to settle disputes and disagreements.

## 2.3. Technical Requirements and Performance Indicators (TRPI)

Technical requirements and performance indicators were incorporated into the concession agreement for five services, namely FEMS, BEMS, CLS, LLS, and CWMS. The objectives of the TRPI were as follows:

- To specify the scope of works
- To follow legal requirements, standards, and manufacturers' recommendations
- To use approved chemical, linen, materials, etc.
- To specify required performance, compliance, and conformance indicators
- To implement a centralized CMIS
- To implement a QAP.

Pertinent aspects of the TRPIs for each service extracted from the CA are illustrated in the appendix, which shows the relationship with the scope of works, the requirements in the contract, and the performance indicators for evaluation purposes.

*FEMS TRPI*

The scope of works of the FEMS TRPI includes the following:

a. To operate, maintain, and monitor engineering plants and central services equipment, like air-conditioning plants, electrical and power substations, pressurized medical gases and vacuums, central steam boilers, water supply, sewerage treatment plants, liquefied petroleum gas (LPG), central sterilization system, fire suppression and detection system, pneumatic tube system, building automatic systems, communication systems, lifts, vehicles, kitchen and office equipment, etc.

b. To provide the facility (workshop), manpower (expertise), tools, equipment, and spare parts in the execution of maintenance and repair of all plants, engineering services, and equipment belonging to the hospital under facility engineering and meeting all stipulated requirements in the TRPI and the MAP, as well as other regulatory requirements of Malaysian law

c. To establish and implement a fault reporting, work requisition, and feedback system

d. To institute and maintain a QAP

e. To provide, implement, and maintain a CMIS

f. To undertake other core activities, such as the following:

    i. Maintenance of M&E fixtures and fittings – planned preventive maintenance, breakdown and repair, inspection, and calibration

    ii. Maintenance of landscapes and pest control

    iii. Witness testing and commissioning of plants and equipment

    iv. Warranty management for new equipment and facilities

    v. Safety and user training, such as fire drills and correct use of equipment and facilities

g. To provide technical advice to the hospital regarding reimbursable and non-reimbursable works

h. To set up and maintain a technical library by procuring all drawings and relevant operational and maintenance documents from consultants and contractors.

Facility-maintenance-related activities (apart from those listed above) to be provided by the concession company are as follows:

- Repair of roof leaks
- Touch-up paint work

- Patching of roads and parking areas
- Clearing of drains and gutters
- Cutting grass
- Irrigation of plants, and weed removal
- Pruning of trees
- Removal of litter and rubbish from roads and compounds
- Repair of fences and gates
- Cleaning blockages in basins, toilet bowls, floor traps, and sewer systems
- Replacing lamp bulbs, fluorescent tubes, starters, and chokes
- Cleaning of ceiling fans, lamp diffusers, and air conditioning diffusers/ grilles
- Repairing electrical appliances
- Repairing furniture and joinery fittings
- Repairing beds, trolleys, wheelchairs, and allied equipment
- Repairing doors and windows
- Changing of gas cylinders in manifold rooms
- Receipts of liquid oxygen, gas cylinders, and fuel oils
- Controlling pests, including disease-bearing insects
- Treating water for cooling towers and the boiler plant (including treatment for legionella)
- Repairing and replacing sanitary fittings (cisterns, toilet seats, taps, shower heads, traps, brackets, etc.)
- Repairing and replacing all ironmongery, including locks
- Maintaining plant/flower nursery
- Rotating potted plants internally
- Moving potted plants from nursery to function point

*BEMS TRPI*

The scope of works for BEMS TRPI includes the following:

- Provide facility, manpower (expertise), tools, equipment, and spare parts in the execution of maintenance and repair of biomedical equipment belonging to the hospital. Standards and procedures must meet all stipulated requirements of the TRPI and MAP, as well as other accepted international/Emergency Care Research Institute (ECRI) standards and guidelines. This safety requirement is in accordance with IEC 601, MS 838, for radiological equipment, and relevant standards for nuclear and radiotherapy equipment

- To provide mechanisms to avoid failure or breakdown during diagnosis or therapy
- To carry out all works necessary to provide uptime guarantee on maintenance
- To provide effective and responsive maintenance, on-call services, and emergency services on all medical equipment and laboratory equipment
- To carry out acceptance testing as well as safety and performance characteristics on all incoming/new biomedical equipment
- To establish and implement a fault-reporting work requisition and feedback system
- To establish a library of user and service manuals
- To undertake other core activities, such as the following:

  - Carry out planned preventive maintenance (PPM) and corrective maintenance
  - Attend to breakdowns and on-call emergencies
  - Carry out and/or participate in safety, performance, and acceptance testing for equipment and outputs
  - Provide witness testing and commissioning of new equipment
  - Provide warranty management for new equipment and facilities
  - Undertake safety and user training, such as in the correct use of equipment
  - Provide technical advice to user

- To dispose of and remove unwanted medical equipment
- To institute and maintain a QAP
- To implement procedures for dealing with hazardous material and handling contaminated equipment
- To cooperate in the investigation of related incidents
- To train users on daily maintenance procedures, excluding clinical procedures, relating to the equipment
- To maintain a stock of genuine spare parts

*CLS TRPI*

The scope of works for the CLS TRPI includes the following:

- To provide manpower, equipment, and supply of all consumable items used in cleansing activities
- To clean areas, including wards, clinics, lobbies, operating theatres, laboratories, pharmacies and allied areas, common areas, corridors, staircases, hospital kitchens, canteens, toilets, housemen's and nurses' quarters, etc.
- To conform to frequencies, standards, procedures, and guidelines in accordance with the TRPI and MAP, and other requirements set by the Ministry of Health (MOH) for cleansing

  - Disinfection and Sterilization Policy and Practice, MOH (1994)
  - Universal Infection Control Precautions, MOH, standard *kebersihan* (cleanliness)
  - Guideline on the Control of Hospital-Acquired Infection by the Medical Service Division of MOH
  - Code of Practice for the Prevention of Infections and Accidents in Hospital Laboratories and Post-Mortem Rooms (1987)

- To make a collection of general waste, which includes the supply of bins from point of generation and transport of the general waste to the central storage facility so that such hospital waste may be disposed of by the local municipality council
- To comply with the standards for the facility, equipment, tools, and consumables set by the MOH which pertain to mops, buckets, vacuum cleaner, polisher, floor stripper, waste bin, garbage bags, trolleys, chemicals/disinfectants, toilet paper, paper hand towels, central garbage bins/house, etc.

*LLS TRPI*

The scope of works for the LLS TRPI includes the following:

- To provide manpower, plant, and equipment, and to supply all linen items used in hospitals as per the hospital-specific list of linens

- To transport clean linen to the contract hospitals and used linen to the off-site laundry facilities/plants
- To supply sufficient clean linen quantity to the wards measured in par:

  - Patient based – two in store and one in use
  - Non-patient – one in store and one in use
  - Special areas – rate of use

- Washing, thermal infection, and finishing shall conform to the United Kingdom Fabric Care Research Association (FCRA) Handbook or equivalent standards
- Sampling testing of linen, chemicals, and processes shall conform to FCRA's standards, including testing for whiteness, chemical residue, tensile strength, and bacteria count, to ensure the quality of linen and the processes
- To conform to material standards, quality, frequency of delivery of clean linen, and the collection of soiled linen in accordance with the TRPI, the MAP, and other requirements set by the MOH for infection control
- To comply with standards for the facility and equipment, including the central store, satellite stores, washers, dryers, ironers, trolleys, transports, and soiled-linen bags and holders
- To comply with standards for linen items, including blankets, bed sheets, pillowcases, patient and staff *baju* (gowns), towels, curtains, screens, cushion covers, etc.
- To repair and replace damaged linen according to MOH's criteria
- To train hospital users on the care, usage, and storage of linen
- All linen belongs to the concession company

## CWMS TRPI

The scope of works for the CWMS TRPI includes the following:

- To provide manpower for CWMS operations in the hospitals and incineration plants
- To build, invest in, and operate a centralized incinerator plant and associated equipment

- To supply in adequate quantities yellow and blue plastic bags, bag holders, sharps containers, and trolleys/bins
- To collect the waste, store it, and transport it to the Department of Environment (DOE)– approved clinical waste incineration plant for disposal
- To ensure that all processes and procedures follow the requirements stipulated in TRPI and MAP, as well as the regulatory requirements of Malaysian law and the standard/guidelines set by the MOH

  - Environmental Quality Act
  - Guidelines for the Management of Clinical and Related Waste in Hospitals and Healthcare Establishments, MOH (1993)
  - Disinfection and Sterilization Policy and Practice, MOH (1994)
  - Code of Practice for the Prevention of Infections and Accidents in Hospital Laboratories and Post-Mortem Rooms (1987).

Clinical waste[1] is defined in the contract as follows:

- Any waste which consists wholly or partly of human or animal tissue, blood, or other body fluids, excretions, drugs or other pharmaceutical products, swabs, dressings, syringes, needles or other instruments, being waste which unless rendered safe may prove hazardous to any person coming into contact with it; and
- Any other waste arising from medical, nursing, dental, veterinary, pharmaceutical or similar practice, investigation, treatment, care, teaching or research, or the collection of blood for transfusion, being waste which can cause infection to any person coming into contact with it.

## 2.4. Master Agreed Procedures

The second important aspect of the concession agreement was the Master agreed procedure (MAP). The MAP addressed in detail the roles and responsibilities of the contract hospitals, the concession companies (CCs), and the MOH. Each of the sections in the MAP elaborated the objectives, scope, definition, references, responsibilities, procedures, and records.

---

[1]    Source- Health Regulations Northern Ireland 2003

Listed below for the five support services in the CA are the general subtitles in the MAP for each category of HSS:

*FEMS*

- Scope of work
- Takeover and purchase of maintenance equipment and materials
- Takeover of engineering workshops and offices
- Takeover of plant rooms
- Takeover of technical documents
- Maintenance facilities
- Location, identification, and labelling of assets
- Condition appraisal
- User maintenance
- Routine inspections
- Planned preventive maintenance (PPM)
- Corrective maintenance, including routine corrective, breakdown, and emergency maintenance
- Scheduling of corrective maintenance
- Indicating when something is beyond economic repair
- Definition of minor works
- Minor works requested by the Ministry of Health
- Minor works requested by the concession company
- Operation of engineering plant and installation
- Other maintenance-related services
- Variations due to addition, modification, or deletion of grounds, buildings, plant, or equipment
- New equipment procured by the Ministry of Health
- New buildings and facilities constructed and supervised by the Ministry of Health
- User maintenance
- Fire safety
- Occupational Health and Safety Act (1994)
- Quality assurance programme
- Maintenance of computer management information system
- On-site library

*BEMS*

- Biomedical engineering services
- PPM
- Corrective maintenance, including routine corrective, breakdown, and emergency maintenance
- Acceptance testing
- Mechanisms to avoid failure or breakdown during use
- Uptime guarantee
- Quality assurance programme
- Maintenance of computer management information system
- Management of warranties
- Decommissioned medical equipment
- Process for handling hazardous/contaminated equipment
- Stock of genuine spare parts
- On-site library
- Workshop set-up
- Advisory service
- Biomedical minor works

*CLS*

- Scope of works
- General areas for cleaning
- Medical areas for cleaning
- Specialized areas for cleaning
- Intensive-care areas
- Identification of source of generation and type of waste generated
- Segregation of waste
- Management of spillage
- Collection route, including frequency and timing of collection
- Identification of responsible staff
- Sealing and handling of black bags
- Transfer of sealed black bags from on-site bag holders to collection devices
- Lining the general waste bag holder with black bags
- Movement of collection device within hospital
- Central storage for general waste

- Cleaning of on-site bag holders and collection devices at central store
- Health, safety, and housekeeping for cleansing services
- Specification for black bags and on-site storage bag holders
- Basic standards of cleanliness
- Definition and process of cleaning

*LLS*

- Purchase of existing linen stock from contract hospitals
- Purchase of new linen
- Purchase of existing laundry equipment
- Takeover of existing contract hospital laundries (if applicable)
- Operation of on-site laundries (if applicable)
- Transport of clean linen
- Storage of clean linen at the contract hospital's central store
- Delivery of clean linen to user store
- Storage of linen at user stores
- Rejection of linen
- Emergency requisitions
- Bagging of soiled linen
- Handling of infectious linen
- Collection of soiled linen from user areas
- Transport of soiled linen from user areas to central holding area
- Repairs of linen
- Replacement of linen
- Processing of linen
- Occupational Safety and Health Act (OSHA)
- Quality assurance programme
- Computer management information system
- Linen loss

*CWMS*

- CWMS specification
- Definition of clinical waste
- Segregation and storage of clinical waste
- Collection of clinical waste
- Management of spillage within contract hospital

- Disinfection of infectious waste
- Recording of waste collected at source of generation
- Sealing, weighing, and documenting clinical waste to be transported for incineration
- Management of spillage on public road
- Loading and storage of clinical waste prior to incineration
- Weighing and documenting of waste received at incineration plant
- Compliance testing of incineration
- Commissioning of incineration plant
- Incineration operation
- Investigation in case consignment note was not received by MOH after one month
- Monitoring and record-keeping for incineration plants having a capacity greater than 1,000 kg per day
- Monitoring and record-keeping for incineration plants having a capacity of 1,000 kg per day or less
- Health, safety, and housekeeping at incineration plant
- Management of ash
- Contingency plan for power failure and plant breakdown and maintenance
- Identification of source of generation and type of waste
- Specification for light blue bag or yellow bag
- Specification for on-site storage bin (bag holder)
- Specification for sharps containers
- Specification of receptacles (for treatment trolley)
- Specification of one-way plastic seal
- Specification of clinical waste collection trolley
- Specification of wheeled bin (storage bin) for transportation of waste
- Central storage area for clinical waste
- Vehicles for transporting clinical waste
- Monthly and yearly performance report on plant operation for submission to MOH

## 2.5. Hospital-Specific Implementation Plan (HSIP)

The third important component of the concession agreement was the drafting of the hospital-specific implementation plan (HSIP) for each hospital covered by the contract. This document was not specifically written in the original contract but was to be written separately in each hospital after the signing of the CA contract, as each hospital has its uniqueness, differentiating it from each and every other hospital.

This HSIP is a document that lists in detail the complete operation of the five support services in each hospital by naming the specific set of tasks and the resources, supplies, and deliverables required of the concession companies. It is a working manual to inform the hospital of what services are provided and when and how the services are to be provided.

The HSIP was derived from the TRPI, the MAP, and specific requirements of the concession agreement. The TRPI specifies performance standards for each of the hospital support services, whereas the MAP specifies the roles and responsibilities of hospital users and the CCs, and the procedures for how the services were to be provided.

The HSIP also provides sufficient details and descriptions of the activities/ deliverables to enable efficient management of the day-to-day operation of the services and the assessment of service performance by the hospital, SIHAT, and the CCs. The HSIP is a reference and resource document for administering and monitoring the support services undertaken by the CCs and the hospital. It is a dynamic document, meaning that revisions can be made throughout the year after approval, and then on a yearly basis. The reasons for the changes could be alterations, additions, omissions, or modifications to the physical assets; higher performance standards required by the end users; changes to statutory requirements or government policies; or changes proposed by the CC to improve the service quality.

The list of items included in the HSIP is as follows:

- Name of hospital
- Address of hospital
- Capacity of the hospital (number of beds)
- Organizational structure of the hospital, including the hospital director, heads of department, and officer in charge of each of the hospital support services of FEMS, BEMS, CLS, LLS, and CWMS

- Organizational structure of the concession company at the hospital, which includes the facility manager and the officers in charge of each the five support services
- Detailed information of the CC's personnel in the hospital, especially critical personal, e.g. electrical chargeman
- Plan of the hospital showing the locations of the various buildings and departments, stores, holding stations, etc.
- Telephone and communication information
- List of assets within the hospital which form part of the contract for maintenance
- List of user locations
- Incorporation of important procedures for service deliveries
- Technical training schedule for the hospital staff for the year
- Schedule of services to be provided
- Schedule of planned preventive maintenance and corrective maintenance, particularly for FEMS and BEMS equipment
- Approved forms/records/reports and names of authorized personnel to sign off work done
- Exemption list of equipment that will not be maintained in the contract
- Number of areas, which affects the parameters in the deduction formula
- List of equipment determined to be beyond economic repair
- List of testing equipment available and due for calibration
- Fire drill schedule
- Communication channels, especially for complaints
- Contingency plans for emergencies or breakdowns
- List of chemicals for cleaning that are approved by the hospital.

HSIP documents are normally prepared by the CCs towards the end of each year and submitted to the hospitals for approval in November of each year. Ideally, the hospitals vet through the documents and give approval before 31 December of each year so that the CC is able to plan its works and schedules for the following year.

In the schedules of delivery for FEMS and BEMS, the PPM schedules make reference to manufacturers' service manuals. In the event that such a manual is not available, reference is made to the Facility Engineering Planned Maintenance Guidelines developed by MOH. In the execution of the PPM, the CC gives two weeks' advance notice to the end users so as not to disrupt their operations.

As for housekeeping services like CLS, LLS, and CWMS, the schedules are discussed and mutually agreed on between the end users and the CCs. Usually, the frequency of the services to be delivered is reasonable.

Standard procedures for the provision of each of the HSS are specified in the MAP. End users and the CCs discuss and agree on procedures specific to the hospital. Some of the common specific procedures that are applied in the execution of the contract are as follows:

- When the hospital invokes an emergency clause to procure third-party services
- How clinical waste is transported from the user's location to the storage areas
- Where and how clinical waste bins are washed
- How and where clean linen is weighed before being sent to user locations
- How soiled linen is transported from the user location to the linen store.

In the signing off for work done, the hospital assigns authorized personnel to the task. This is especially applicable for work orders for PPM, clean linen requests (CLR), clean linen issue notes (CLIN), the clinical waste requisition sheet (CWRS), CLS daily cleaning activity (DCA), and joint inspection (JI).

Contingency plans are incorporated with the HSIP so that users and CCs can mitigate situations appropriately in case of interruptions in HSS. The causes of the interruption could be utility failure, such as power or air-conditioning failure in operating theatres, the intensive-care unit, the coronary care unit, or the pharmacy. CWMS and laundry plant failures are a concern as well, as the failure could cause backlogs.

An exemption list for equipment requiring maintenance is submitted by the CCs so that the equipment is exempted from meeting the TRPI and MAP standards in the contract. Before exemption is granted, the CCs submit their proposals to the hospitals with the explanation. Both the hospital and the state health department verify and approve the application. Prior to exemption, the CCs pay the maintenance fee in full. Thus, a deadline must be instituted for the repair of items on the exemption list.

## 2.6. Deduction Formula (DF)

As it is not possible to capture every detail in the deduction formula's process because of its complexity, this section only provides a summary of the salient points for the deduction formulation, namely methodology, indicators, parameters, data sources for demerit points, application process, and validation process.

The idea of the deduction formula arose because there was a need to institute a process of making payment to the contractor. The mode of payment as drafted in the CA is by fixed amount on a yearly schedule for FEMS, BEMS, and CLS. For LLS and CWMS, it is by kilograms for soiled linen and waste respectively. The fee is negotiated and agreed on by the government of Malaysia and the CC before the award of the contract. The period of the contract is for fifteen years. For ease of administering the project, the yearly schedule is divided into monthly fees and paid progressively. The deduction formula is a mutually agreed on formula between the government and the CC to address issues of non-conformance by the CC, as stipulated in the technical requirements performance indicators (TRPI).

Basically, the DF is composed in the following way:

- Each of the five services has its own set of performance indicators that are used to monitor the respective scope and service standards.
- Each performance indicator is accorded a specific number of demerit points based on the relative importance to performance and on conformance to the scope and service standards.
- Demerit points are imposed for each episode of non-performance of or non-conformance to a particular performance indicator, and the demerit points for each performance indicator are accumulated for the month.
- Based on the total number of demerit points, a sum of money is deducted from the fees payable to the CC.
- The sum to be deducted from the monthly fees payable to the CC is the total accumulated demerit points for the month multiplied by a ringgit equivalent value for each demerit point, an example of which is provided below.

Total sum to be deducted = Total accumulated demerit points × ringgit equivalent

- The performance indicator, the number of demerit points for each and every performance indicator, and the ringgit value for each demerit point is determined through mutual agreement between the government and the CC.

## 2.6.1. Methodology of Deduction

Application of the methodology of deduction is divided into two parts, namely Part A and Part B. Part A consist of a key deduction indicator where routine activities generally are requested or scheduled and carried out monthly and, thus, assessments are made on monthly activities. Part B consists of key indicators where assessment is carried out periodically and is assessed for an assessment period.

The ratio or weightage of the monthly service fee (or total service for the corresponding assessment period) of the two parts is tabulated typically in Table 1, below. Table 2, below, shows the timetable for the assessment of the periodic deduction for Part B.

Table 1 **Weightage for monthly service fee**

| Service | Part A (%) | Part B (%) |
|---|---|---|
| 1. Facility engineering maintenance services (FEMS) | 80 | 20 |
| 2. Biomedical engineering management services (BEMS) | 80 | 20 |
| 3. Cleansing services (CLS) | 95 | 5 |
| 4. Linen and laundry services (LLS) | 80 | 20 |
| 5. Clinical waste management services (CWMS) | 85 | 15 |

Table 2 **Timetable for assessment of periodic deduction for Part B**

| Assessment period | Month | Month of assessment |
|---|---|---|
| 1. Quarterly | January to March | April |
| | April to June | July |
| | July to September | October |
| | October to December | January |
| 2. Semi-annually | January to June | July |
| | July to December | January |
| 3. Annually | January to December | January |

A gearing factor (GF) was introduced to reflect the degree and magnitude of individual non-conformances by the CC. This gearing factor is a multiplication factor imposed on accumulated demerit points to differentiate the level of each non-conformance based on either selected equipment (or systems for FEMS) or user departments (for CLS and LLS).

Should there be a recurrence of similar non-conformances, the multiplication factor is compounded (if applicable) with the accumulated demerit points. This recurrence is called the recurrence factor (RF). This factor is applicable irrespective of whether the non-conformance is normal or critical. This factor is compounded by the recurrence of similar non-conformances, such as breakdowns, PPM of the same equipment, linen shortfalls, and non-conformance of work. For FEMS and BEMS, a similar breakdown of the same asset should not recur within a fixed period from the last similar breakdown. The RF takes into account uncompleted PPM, routine inspection (RI), and scheduled corrective maintenance (SCM) brought forward from the previous month(s) as recurrence. Recurrence of non-conformances in CLS and LLS are taken on a daily basis until the end of the month.

A gearing ratio (GR) is compounded with the accumulated demerit points due to non-conformance in critical departments/areas in addition to the gearing factor and the recurrence factor (if applicable) for FEMS and BEMS.

## 2.6.2. The Deduction Formula

The calculation of the deduction formula is described below.

Indicator value (RM)  = Monthly service fee × indicator weightage
Ringgit equivalent (RM) = Indicator value for the month or assessment period
Parameter  = Number of service requests for the month
Deduction value  = Ringgit equivalent × total demerit points

Total demerit points = Sum of (DP + GF + RF + GR)
Where  DP = Demerit point
   GF = Gearing factor
   RF = Recurrence factor
   GR = Gearing ratio

**Worked Example of Deduction Formula**

The formula below is based on facility engineering maintenance services for a key deduction indicator with a weightage of 0.6.

Indicator value for the month = Total monthly service fee × weightage
   = RM900, 000 × 0.06
   = RM54, 000

Parameter   = Number of service requests for the month
   (excluding PPM)
   = 770

Ringgit equivalent  = Indicator value for the month
            Parameter
   = RM54, 000/770
   = RM70.13 per month

Deduction value  = Ringgit equivalent × number of demerit points
   = RM70.13 × 40
   = RM2, 805.19 per month

*Assuming the number of demerit points = 40*

Tables 3 and 4, below, summarize the typical calculation of a deduction for Part A and Part B.

### Table 3  **Part A – Monthly service fee**

| No. | Indicator | Indicator weightage | Indicator value | Parameters | Ringgit equivalent | Demerit points | Deduction |
|-----|-----------|---------------------|-----------------|------------|--------------------|----------------|-----------|
| (A) | (B) | (C) | (D)=(C)× MF | (E) | (F)=(D)/(E) | (G) | (H)=(F)×(G) |
| | | | | | | | |
| | | | | | | Total deduction= | |

MF = Monthly fee

### Table 4  **Part B – Total fee for assessment period**

| No. | Indicator | Indicator weightage | Indicator value | Parameters | Ringgit equivalent | Demerit points | Deduction |
|-----|-----------|---------------------|-----------------|------------|--------------------|----------------|-----------|
| (A) | (B) | (C) | (D)=(C)× MF | (E) | (F)=(D)/(E) | (G) | (H)=(F)×(G) |
| | | | | | | | |
| | | | | | | Total deduction= | |

TF = Total monthly fee for assessment period
(annual, semi-annual, or quarterly)

Note: Where applicable, demerit points (DP) shall be multiplied with the related gearing factor (GF) and gearing ratio (GR).

## 2.6.3. Key Deduction Indicators

Each of the services has its own key deduction indicators. In summary, they are as follows:

*FEMS*

- Functioning facility engineering systems
- PPM, RI, and scheduled corrective maintenance completed
- PPM, RI, and scheduled corrective maintenance completed on schedule

- Appropriate response time on all service-request work orders lodged by hospitals
- Service requests completed within stipulated time (two weeks)
- Statutory requirements and calibration certificate requirements met
- Participation in testing and commissioning of new equipment and engineering systems
- Providing appropriate technical advice to hospital about the performance of engineering systems
- Timely submission of technical reports and condition appraisals of equipment/systems
- Accurate and updated data to the CMIS
- User training conducted according to schedule
- Compliance with a quality assurance programme

*BEMS*

- All registered equipment functioning in good and safe working order
- All scheduled PPM and RI completed according to agreed schedule
- All scheduled corrective maintenance completed according to agreed schedule
- Appropriate response time for all service-request work orders lodged
- All required data and reports in the CMIS entered daily and updated within twenty-four hours after work completion
- All maintenance related service-request work orders completed within seven days
- User training completed according to schedule
- QAP process implemented for the agreed indicator, and asset type; indicator standard set to be achieved and reported accordingly
- Compliance with TRPI and MAP of technical service performance audit outcome on the biomedical engineering maintenance system and/or its component
- Statutory requirements, calibration certificate requirements, and condition appraisal recommendations met
- Technical advice requirements and condition appraisal provided as per mandatory requirement
- Uptime target for assets and equipment in compliance with TRPI
- Testing, commissioning, and warranty management of newly introduced equipment/system carried out promptly

## CLS

- Outcome of cleansing activities meets good quality standards.
- Cleansing carried out at all user areas
- Cleansing carried out at user areas according to agreed schedule
- Cleansing activities carried out following the agreed procedures
- Sufficient supplies of consumables provided and replenished at all user areas
- Collection of general waste
- Collection of general waste as per schedule
- Chemicals and equipment used approved by the MOH
- Reports and records submitted on time
- Accurate and correct reports and records

## LLS

- Clean and acceptable linen delivered
- Adequate acceptable linen delivered as required
- Adequate acceptable linen delivered on time
- Soiled linen collected on time
- All applicable statutory requirements complied with
- All records and reports submitted on time
- Accurate and correct reports and records

## CWMS

- Adequate supply of bags and containers provided
- Collection of clinical waste (CW) carried out
- Collection of CW carried out as per schedule using clean, dry trolleys
- Waste collected and stored without being mixed with non-MOH waste?
- CW store properly maintained
- Reports and records submitted on time
- CW transported away according to schedule
- User training done according to schedule
- Compliance with all legal requirements
- Accurate and correct reports and records

## 2.6.4. Parameters Used for the Indicators

Parameters used for the five services are as follows:

*FEMS*

- Number of systems × user locations × days for the month
- Number of assets not included in systems × days for the month
- PPM, RI, and scheduled corrective maintenance for the month
- Number of assets, personnel required, and systems required for the month in order to be in legal compliance
- Number of training sessions scheduled for the month
- Number of testing and commissioning sessions scheduled for the month
- Number of technical requests for the month
- Number of service requests for the month
- Number of reports and records submitted for the month

*BEMS*

- Number of pieces of equipment and number of personnel for the month
- Number of user trainings scheduled for the month
- Number of testing and commissioning sessions scheduled for the month
- Number of service requests for the month
- Number of reports and records submitted for the month
- Number of instances of PPM and work requests, including corrective maintenance, for the month where safety and performance tests are required
- Total number of applicable records
- Service requests for the month plus requests not closed for the previous months

*CLS*

- Total number of joint inspections for the month
- Total number of user locations inspected
- Total number of demerit points due to application of GF and RF where applicable

- Total number of consumables
- Total number of receptacles
- Number of pieces of equipment, number of tools, and amount of chemicals used by the hospital
- Number of reports and records submitted for the month

*LLS*

- Quantity requested for the month
- Number of bags collected for the month
- Number of pieces of equipment and number of personnel required for the month in order to be in legal compliance
- Number of reports and records submitted for the month

*CWMS*

- Number of user locations × days for the month
- Number of stores × days for the month
- Number of user locations plus central store × days of the month
- Number of reports and records submitted for the month
- Number of collections for the month
- Number of user training sessions for the month
- Number of certificates, licenses, and consignment notes for the month

## 2.6.5. Data Sources for Demerit Point Computations

Data sources for the computation of demerit points are derived from many sources, but mainly from the CMIS, automatically generated complaints, other complaints, non-conformance reports (NCR), joint inspections, HSIPs, samples of data, records, etc. Demerit points are then derived from a combination of the non-conformances from the CMIS, hospital complaints, and NCRs from SIHAT. Samples of records are taken to verify data entry to CMIS against hard copies of work orders, delivery and collection forms, records, etc.

CMIS are used where possible and are applicable for generating demerit points (automatic complaint generation (ACG) for some of the indicators). Complaints are mainly lodged by hospital staff.

NCRs are generated through inspection by SIHAT and the CC, which includes checking information against the HSIP, samples of data and records, etc. Photographs to serve as evidence of non-conformance are taken and filed.

## 2.6.6. Deduction Application and Validation Process

The deduction application and validation process is as follows:

- The contractor, from the MIS, confirms that the complaint/NCR is a complaint and is not duplicated
- The contractor maps the NCRs/complaints to the indicators (CMIS – financial and deduction report)
- SIHAT takes samples of rejected complaints to verify the correctness of the MIS, confirmation, and mapping
- The contractor either accepts the confirmed complaints/NCRs or provides evidence to the validation committee
- Mapping report – accepted demerit points are forwarded to hospital/SIHAT not later than the seventh day of the subsequent month
- The contractor provides evidence to the hospital committee of any complaints/NCRs not accepted no later than the fifteenth day of the subsequent month
- The hospital committee meets as necessary throughout the month, with the final meeting to be held no later than the twenty-first day of the month
- The contractor provides a final list of demerit points to SIHAT before the twenty-third day of the month
- SIHAT issues a deduction assessment before the end of the month
- Deduction based on demerit points is made to the subsequent month's invoice
- Any matters which could not be resolved by the hospital committee are referred to the state committee, which includes representatives of the state health department, the hospital, the MOH, SIHAT, and the contractor.

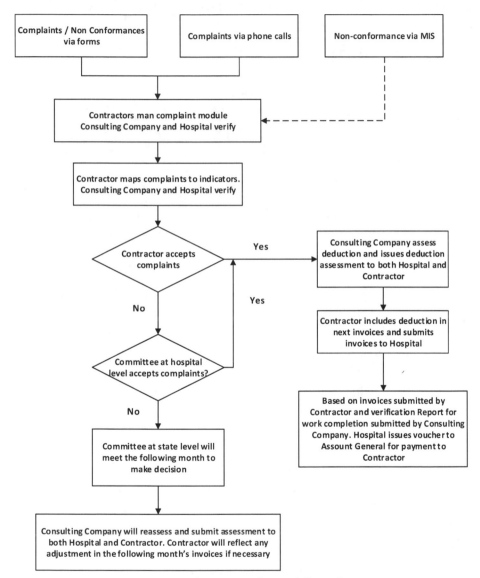

Figure 3 **Deduction application flow chart**

## 2.7. Third-Party Clauses

The use of third-party clauses in the contract agreement is essential to ensuring that hospital services are not neglected and jeopardized. The extract of the third-party clauses is as follows:

- The government's right to procure third-party services
- Notice of emergency
- Immediate diagnosis and/or treatment of patients

*The Government's Right to Procure Third-Party Services*

This clause is to provide the government the right to procure the services of a third party when the CC has failed to perform the service according to the contract agreement. An extract of the clause[2] is given below:

- The Government reserves the right but shall not be obliged to engage any other party to carry out any part of the Services which the CC has failed or neglected to carry out and remedy in accordance with this Agreement.
- The costs of engaging any such party to carry out the Services shall be borne by the CC and may, at the discretion of the Government be deducted from monies due to the CC from the Government.
- Save and except in situations of emergencies, the Government shall not exercise its rights under this Clause without first giving the CC, not less than fourteen (14) days written notice of its intention to do so.
- In the event that t the CC remedies such failure or neglect to the satisfaction of the Government within the fourteen (14) days period, the Government shall not engage any other party to carry party to carry out such part of the Services.

Conditions justifying the application of this clause are as follows:

- Failure of any part of the service and/or neglect to remedy the failure
- Should not be use as the norm (an exception)
- Written notification must be issued

---

[2]   Source: Concession Agreement between Government of Malaysia and Companies Oct 1996

- Could be issued any time after a complaint or service request is lodged, with fourteen days given to the CC to remedy before implementation by contract hospital
- Agreement or consent by CC is not a prerequisite
- Payment by deduction of fee
- Not applicable for approved exemption/beyond economic repair (BER) list items
- Procurement of services should follow current treasury instructions or procedures.

This clause applies to the following:

- Maintenance and repair of facility and biomedical engineering systems, facilities, and equipment
- Preventive maintenance
- Purchase of laundry services and linen items
- Purchase of cleansing services and collection of waste (clinical and domestic) as well as consumables items (partly or wholly)
- Purchase of maintenance spare parts.

*Notice of Emergency*

The notice of emergency clause is to be applied to emergency situations which affect the services to be provided to the hospitals and to life-threatening situations which require alternative solutions, usually from third-party providers. This clause[3] stipulates as follows:

> If an emergency occurs, the CC shall forthwith notify the Government's Representative of the emergency and the operating actions taken. Following such notification, at the request of the Government's Representative, the Parties shall discuss without delay the further actions which should be taken as a result of the emergency.

---

[3]     Source: Concession Agreement between Government of Malaysia and Companies Oct 1996

i.   If the Government's Representative considers that an emergency has arisen in relation to a Contract Hospital in providing the Services the Government Representative may inform the CC of the nature of the emergency which he has identified and the manner in which he requests such emergency to be rectified

ii.  The CC shall rectify such defect with all due diligence. If the CC fails to comply with such notice promptly the Government shall be entitled to procure that it or any third party takes such action as may be necessary to remedy such breach by the CC. All reasonable cost and expenses in respect of the works required for the provision of the Service that have been carried out by the third party shall be reimbursed by the CC.

The conditions giving rise to notice of emergency are as follows:

- Emergency situation in relation to the services at the hospital, and contractor failure to respond to the notice
- Should not be use as the norm (exception)
- Written notice of the intention to the CC and no window period
- Applicable to all five services
- Agreement or consent by the CC not a prerequisite at any time in the event of emergency or life-threatening situation
- Payment to be reimbursed by the CC
- Not applicable for approved exemption/BER list items
- Procurement of services shall follow current treasury instructions or procedures

This clause applies to the following:

- Emergency repair of facility and biomedical engineering (facilities, systems, and equipment)
- Emergency purchase of laundry services
- Emergency purchase of linen items for immediate use
- Emergency purchase of services for the purpose of patient treatment and care, for example:

  ➢ Transportation costs or other expenses incurred during ambulance breakdown

&#10147; Sending of central sterile supply department (CSSD) utensils to another MOH/private facility for autoclaving.

## *Immediate Diagnosis and/or Treatment of Patients*

This clause is for patients who require immediate diagnosis or treatment where the medical equipment has broken down and who need to be sent to a nearby medical facility with similar equipment for diagnosis or treatment. The clause[4] stipulates as follows:

- If the Hospital Director of any Contract Hospital considers that immediate diagnoses and/or treatment of a patient is necessary as a result of failure or breakdown of the provision of the Services and/or the installed Facility, then the Government shall be entitled to send the said patient for similar diagnoses and/or treatment at any medical facility available.
- Subject to the provisions of defects and defaults of the Government as stated in the contract, all costs and expenses incurred by the Government shall be reimbursed by the CC.

The conditions for the application of this clause are as follows:

- Emergency situation where the patient requires immediate diagnosis/ treatment
- Failure or breakdown of service delivery/installed facility
- Should not be use as the norm (an exception)
- Written notice of the intention to the CCs
- Not meant to reduce current and backlog workload
- Not applicable for approved exemption/BER list items
- Payment reimbursement by CC.

This clause applies to the following:

- Purchase of radiology services
- Purchase of laboratory services
- Patient treatment such as haemodialysis

---

4 Source: Concession Agreement between Government of Malaysia and Companies Oct 1996

## 2.8. HSS Quality Assurance Programme (QAP)

Part of the CC's obligations in the contract is to provide a quality assurance programme (QAP) in the execution of the HSS contract for all five services. The contract stipulates that the CC initiate a QAP for the services in order to achieve ISO 9002:1993-"*Model for Quality Assurance in production, installation and service*" registration within five years from the takeover date and to maintain the registration throughout the concession period. The requirements are incorporated in the TRPI and the MAP.

However, this programme was not fully executed at the beginning of the project, as the clarity of execution was vague. All three appointed CCs had their own approaches, so there was incoordination and confusion in the implementation of the QAP. In the year 1999, the MOH appointed SIHAT to spearhead a programme concerned with the proper development and implementation of the HSS QAP for all of MOH's hospitals. A series of meetings, pilot studies, and projects were organized with the goal of the proper implementation of this programme, which took effect in 2006.

The objectives of the QAP are as follows:

- To enable the concession company to monitor performance levels against set standards
- To address any shortcomings in the service performance
- To ensure that continuous improvements to the service are provided.

The intention of the QAP was to build a quality culture in the CCs, the MOH, and the hospitals, to fulfil the requirements of the CA and to meet ISO 9001:2008 requirements. The QAP arose out of concerns about the availability of ready-to-use FEMS and BEMS equipment, the availability of clean linen in sufficient quantity, the safe disposal of clinical waste, and a clean and hygienic environment in the hospitals.

In the execution of the QAP, a system of procedures, standards, formulae, requirements, formats of documentation, and organizational structure was developed. The QAP standards and procedures offered a list of standards, indicators, and cause codes that were used as key references throughout the concession period. Sixteen indicators were derived for the five services, as shown in Table 5, below.

QAP was a complicating process in the HSS contract. Not all the processes had been implemented over the course of the project due to lack of information and inherent difficulties like the determination of linen loss. Only selected items were implemented, and these were carried out in stages.

Implementation of the indicators was staggered over a period of time as agreed by the MOH. The first phase of full implementation of the programme involved four indicators (two for FEMS (indicators 1 and 2) and two for BEMS (indicators 5 and 6)) out of the sixteen indicators as agreed by the MOH. The second phase involved three other services and additional equipment for FEMS and BEMS as agreed by the MOH. The indicators for the three other services were indicators 7 and 8 for CLS; 10, 11, and 12 for LLS; and 15 and 16 for CWMS.

The rationale for the omission of the other indicators was as follows:

- Indicator 3 did not address the areas of concern for FEMS and BEMS (availability of facilities and biomedical equipment).
- Data on the cancellation of healthcare services was not available from the CC to implement indicator 4.
- Inadequate data or unavailable data on response time to implement indicator 9 as the event (spillage) was ad hoc in nature.
- A linen loss formula had not been agreed on and required further study for implementation of indicator 13.
- Data on needle-stick injury involving hospital personnel were not available from the CC to implement indicator 14.

Table 5 **Indicators and standards**

| Service | Indicators | Description | Standards |
|---|---|---|---|
| FEMS | 1 | Percentage of PPM completed as scheduled per month | 100% |
| | 2 | Percentage of assets meeting uptime target per month | 100% |
| | 3 | Percentage of response times meeting target | 100% |
| | 4 | Number of cancellations of healthcare services per month | 0 |

| BEMS | 5 | Percentage of PPM completed as scheduled per month | 100% |
|------|----|------|------|
| | 6 | Percentage of assets meeting uptime target per month | 100% |
| CLS | 7 | Percentage of acceptable cleansing quality based on joint inspection per month | 95% |
| | 8 | Percentage of general waste collected per month | 95% |
| | 9 | Percentage of compliance to response time target | 100% |
| LLS | 10 | Percentage of acceptable linen per month | 98% |
| | 11 | Percentage of linen issued against request per month | 95% |
| | 12 | Percentage of compliance to linen delivery per month | 100% |
| | 13 | Percentage of linen per month | 0% |
| CWMS | 14 | Incident rate or reported needle-stick injury | 0% |
| | 15 | Percentage of collection of clinical waste per month | 100% |
| | 16 | Percentage of transportation of clinical waste per month | 100% |

## 2.8.1. Organization

The HSS QAPs were organized into six groups, namely the QAP Steering Committee, the QAP project team, the QAP core team, the CC QAP team, the regional or area QAP Team, and the HSS QAP team. Another group of personnel, those who were independent of the activities being verified and audited at the sites, made up the data verification team.

*QAP Steering Committee*

This was the umbrella committee of the HSS QAP. Its chairperson was the director of the Engineering Division of MOH, and members were those of the QAP project team. This committee was responsible for priority determination, strategic planning, HSS QAP review and approval, indicator approval, and standards revision.

*QAP Project Team*

This was the design and development committee of HSS QAP. Its members were representatives of three concession companies' QAP core teams, the Supervision Unit of the Engineering Division of the MOH, and SIHAT. This committee was responsible for the whole HSS QAP design and development, and for periodic review and reporting to the HSS QAP Steering Committee chairperson.

*QAP Core Team*

This was the committee that coordinated cross-functioning and standardization amongst the three CCs. The committee consisted of representatives from each CC QAP team, SIHAT, and the consultant engaged by the CCs. Its meetings were organized on a rotational basis by the CCs.

*CC QAP Team*

This was the coordinating committee at the CC level. It was responsible for implementing QAP within its CC and for facilitating QAP-related training. The typical CC QAP is illustrated below:

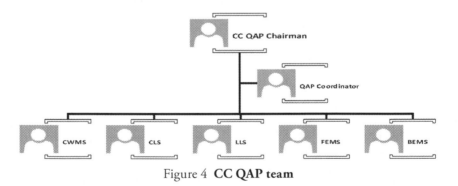

Figure 4 **CC QAP team**

*Regional or Area QAP Team*

The team in the region was headed by the regional manager or area manager. The regional quality, safety, health, and environment executive/facilitator acted as the secretary. The team was responsible for the overall implementation of the QAP in the hospitals and the regional office.

*HSS QAP Team*

This team was the "arms and legs" of HSS QAP that was responsible for implementing the QAP at the hospital level and ensuring the participation of a liaison officer from the hospital. The liaison officer had to be a member of the QA committee of his or her hospital to ensure a coordinated effort in the hospital's overall QAP.

*Data Verification Team*

The responsibility of the data verification team was to ensure the accuracy and reliability of data and to be an independent entity to ensure that data integrity was not compromised. Data integrity ensured the accuracy of data during the data collection process, the data entry process, and the period after the data were entered into the basic MIS.

## 2.8.2. QAP Process

In brief, the HSS QAP process consisted of data collection, identification of shortfalls and cause codes, verification by data verification officers (DVOs), and generation of shortfall in quantity (SIQ) and corrective action report (CAR) to address any non-compliance within a specific time period. These are illustrated in Figures 5 and 6, below.

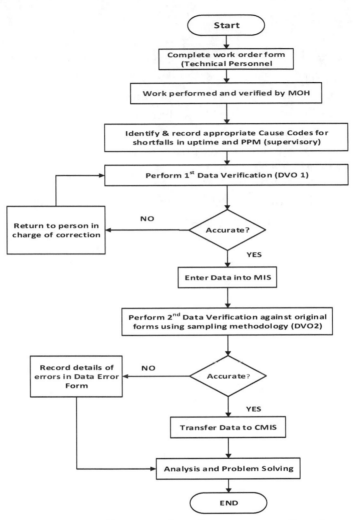

Figure 5  **Data collection and verification process flow chart**

## Process Details for Data Collection and Verification Process Flow

- Technical personnel in charge of the maintenance activity are to identify all maintenance works and to ensure they are executed accordingly. Forms to be verified by MOH staff.
- Supervisor/person in charge of the activities is to identify the proper cause code for each non-conformance in uptime and PPM.
- Data verification officer 1 (DVO1) is to check the completion of the form and sign off to verify completeness and correctness of data. If any detail on a form is found to be incomplete or incorrect, the form

should be returned to the supervisor/person in charge for completion and/or correction.

- Upon verification of the form, the help desk assistant is to key the verified form data in to the CMIS.
- Data verification officer 2 (DVO2) is to check the accuracy of data in the basic MIS screen against the original data source using sampling methodology.
- Upon completion of data verification, the DVO2 is to sign off the sampled source records. If there were errors, the DVO2 is to record the details of the errors in the Data Error forms
- The DVO2 is to submit the Data Error form to the person in charge for correction.

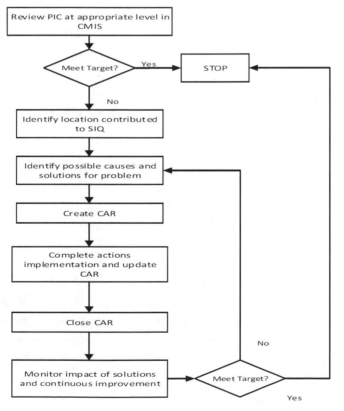

Figure 6 **Data analysis process**

The respective service head at the appropriate level is to assess the QAP's service performance level against the set performance standard on a quarterly basis.

The problem-solving process is applicable when an SIQ is identified for any of the QAP indicators. The team members should use the applicable problem-solving process and problem-solving or quality-management quality assurance/quality control (QA/QC) tools. The selection of tools varies depending on the application; it is up to the user to select the appropriate tools. When the corrective action is completed, results of the semi-annual cycle are evaluated to see if the QAP performance cycle was successful. The corrective actions taken and the results of the corrective action are reported in the semi-annual cycle to the management and MOH.

## 2.9. Reimbursable Works

At the commencement of the project in 1996, there was no clear definition of the works that fell under maintenance and those which required additional inputs and costs to upgrade or to reconstruct. Confusion and disputes arose when hospitals demanded work maintenance with high costs that were assumed not to be part of the CA. To overcome the confusion, a supplementary agreement was introduced in January 2003, to define works that were under maintenance within the ambit of the contract and works that were reimbursable to the contractor.

There were two methods by which reimbursable works could be executed in the hospitals. One was to be initiated by the hospital, whereas the other was to be initiated by the CC. Two clauses were stated in the contract to carry out reimbursable works, which were mainly for FEMS and BEMS, as follows:

a)  The Government may make a written request that the CC carry out Reimbursable Works at a Contract Hospital whereby the Government will specify the nature of the said works. Upon such request, the CC shall submit the estimated costs of such works for the consideration and approval of the Government. If the Government approves such costing the CC shall so carry out the said works with due diligence.

b)  The CC may submit a written recommendation to the Government that Reimbursable Works be carried out at a Contract Hospital. The CC shall provide the Government with information as to the basis of the recommendation, the alternatives available, the costs of the alternatives available, the estimated effect on the present and future operation and maintenance of a Contract Hospital of the various alternatives if implemented and the alternative recommended by the CC. Should the Government approve both the recommended Reimbursable Works and the costs involved, then the Government may allow the CC to carry out the said works.[5]

Prior to proposing any reimbursable works, the CC was to carry out a condition appraisal of the installed facility involved and then submit the report to the hospital and/or MOH for their consideration and approval. Where the reimbursable work was requested by the CC for rectifying damages due to vandalism, theft, misuse, and/or mishandling by the user/patients/hospital personnel, the CC needed to submit written proof of such event, supported by relevant documents such as police reports, and technical reports from qualified personnel.

However, any damages resulting from acts or omission of maintenance were to be rectified by the CC at its own cost and treated as maintenance work.

Table 6 **Examples of maintenance-related and reimbursable works**

| Scope of service | Maintenance related | Reimbursable works |
|---|---|---|
| **FEMS** | | |
| a) Painting of buildings | Touch-up of building and repainting of section(s) of the building | Repainting of the entire building or of the entire location |
| b) Repairs to pitched roof leakage | Repair of roof leakages, including replacement of damaged portions of the roof tiles, roofing sheets, and roof accessories | Replacing the entire roof covering and/or roof truss system of any or all of the building or block |
| | Repair or replacement of damaged or faulty members or sections of the roof truss system. | |

---

5    Source – Concession Agreement between The Government of Malaysia and Companies 1996

| | | | |
|---|---|---|---|
| c) | Sanitary fittings, such as sinks, washbasins, and toilet bowls | Repairs, removal of blockages, and/or replacement of damaged or broken sanitary fittings and/or components such as ball valves, etc. | Upgrading or relocating sanitary fittings as per hospital request<br><br>Replacing sanitary fittings proven to have been damaged by vandalism |
| d) | Electrical fittings | Repair of faulty electrical fittings<br><br>Replacement of faulty bulbs, ballasts, wiring, etc. | Upgrading of the lighting and electrical fittings<br><br>Relocating and/or installing additional power socket outlets and light fixtures |
| e) | Lightning protection and earthing system | Repairs including replacement of missing, damaged, or faulty conductors, air terminals, test clamps, earth chambers, earthing rods, etc. | Replacing the system or component proven to be missing or damaged on account of vandalism or theft<br><br>Upgrading of entire system |
| f) | Air conditioning and ventilation system | Repairs or replacement of faulty, leaking, or damaged ductwork and/or insulation<br><br>Repairs of the system, including replacement of faulty or damaged components such as compressors or pumps<br><br>Replacement of filters<br><br>Duct cleaning and disinfecting<br><br>Load balancing and calibration of control system (for central system) | Replacing, extending, and/or upgrading the entire duct system<br><br>Relocating a portion of the ductwork/system<br><br>Replacing condemned items as per request<br><br>Upgrading the air-conditioning unit or system based on current needs or new standards, or as per user request |
| g) | Medical gases system | Repairs or replacement of faulty or damaged pipes and fittings<br><br>Repairs of medical gases plant and replacement of faulty or damaged components such as manifold, manifold components, pumps, tanks, alarm panel, and terminal units | Replacing, extending, or upgrading of entire system<br><br>Upgrading of various components to meet the current service requirements or new standards/specifications<br><br>Relocating a portion of pipework/system |

| | | |
|---|---|---|
| | Management of statutory compliance including preparation for inspection by regulating agency | Replacing missing components proven to have been damaged by way of vandalism or theft<br><br>Installing additional terminal units or components |
| **BEMS** | | |
| h) Maintenance of biomedical equipment | Repair, including the replacement of spares<br><br>Reinstatement of deleted or corrupted software<br><br>Supply of maintenance-related consumables such as calibration fluid, electrodes, and X-ray films for calibration<br><br>Replacement of various types of bulbs, fuses, batteries, suction bottles, probes, cables, lead wires for electrodes, vacuum components, reusable electrodes and filters, etc.<br><br>Management of warranty maintenance services | Modifying/upgrading the entire equipment/system (including the operating and application software) to meet new standards/ specifications or new use at the request of the hospital/MOH authorities<br><br>Replacing damaged/broken/ faulty biomedical instruments that do not require PPM/ accessories, subject to approval of hospital authorities<br><br>Replacing items that have been damaged by the user (accidental/ mishandling), a patient, and/ or vandalism, which has to be proven by the CC and approved by the hospital/MOH<br><br>Dismantling of and/or relocating to approved site decommissioned and condemned biomedical equipment/system (installed as part of the room/building)<br><br>Pre-installing works for newly purchased equipment for which the supply contract has no provision for the installation works<br><br>Supplying and installing any items not covered under the warranty or purchase agreement |

# Chapter 3

# Hospital Support Services

Five hospital support services will be discussed in this chapter, as these form the services for the concession contract. These fives services are facilities engineering maintenances services (FEMS), biomedical engineering maintenance services (BEMS), cleansing services (CLS), laundry and linen services (LLS), and clinical waste management services (CWMS).

## 3.1. Facilities Engineering Maintenance Services (FEMS)

### 3.1.1. General

Facilities engineering maintenance services (FEMS) is the field focusing on the design, construction, and life-cycle maintenance of equipment, installations, buildings, and civil works. It involves all facets of life-cycle management, from planning through disposal – including design, construction, environmental protection, site operations, and support.

In the concession agreement (CA), FEMS involves the disciplines of mechanical and electrical engineering, civil engineering, and architecture, including buildings and ground. Biomedical engineering is not included.

### 3.1.2. Scope of Works

Essentially, the FEMS scope of works in the CA as described in the TRPI consists of the following:

a) Maintenance of mechanical and electrical engineering system and plant, civil engineering works, and grounds

b) Operation of all engineering plants and installations
c) Carrying out of minor works
d) Providing technical advice related to the operation and maintenance of buildings and engineering facilities and to reimbursable and non-reimbursable works in the hospitals

Additional works included are the following:

e) Setting up of a technical library
f) Establishing and implementing a fault-reporting, work-requisition, and feedback system
g) Witness testing and commissioning of plants and equipment
h) Providing warranty management to new equipment and facilities
i) Instituting and maintaining a quality assurance programme (QAP)
j) Maintaining landscape and doing pest control.

## 3.1.3. Specific Goals of FEMS

The specific goals of FEMS are as follows:

- To prolong the life and improve the capacity of the facilities to perform at their optimal potential
- To reduce operating interruptions and failures while the assets are in use, particularly those supplying energy to critical areas and life support equipment
- To increase the productivity and skill level of the operation and maintenance (O&M) personnel and improve the works methods and procedures
- To operate the plant and systems in the healthcare facility in a cost-effective and efficient manner
- To reduce the risk of fire and other hazards
- To maintain the entire facility to optimum operating conditions, ensuring that patient care requirements are not compromised
- To maintain the aesthetic qualities of the facilities so as to ensure maximum comfort to the patients of, visitors to, and staff of the healthcare facility.

## 3.1.4. Asset Life Cycle

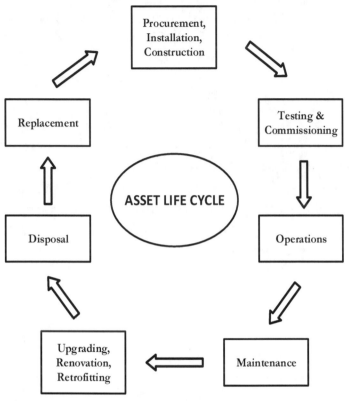

Figure 7 **Asset life cycle**

The asset life cycle diagram is given in Figure 7, above. It is known that every piece of equipment, every installation, and every building has to go through these phases in the life cycle, from procurement/installation/construction to testing and commissioning, operations, maintenance, upgrading/renovating/ retrofitting, disposal, and replacement. FEMS must take note of all these important phases in order to effectively manage the assets to their fullest operational capacities.

## 3.1.5. Testing and Commissioning

Testing and commissioning is defined as the process of ensuring that systems are designed, installed, functionally tested, and capable of being operated and maintained to perform as they were designed and intended to perform.

Thus, in the CA, testing and commissioning (T&C) was an important aspect of FEMS activity. It marked the time when the concession company (CC) would be taking over the asset for operation and maintenance. As such, the CC had to ensure that the T&C was carried out properly so that the equipment would be set correctly and properly, according to parameters, before handing it over to the hospital. Any defects detected were to be highlighted and documented for the vendors or suppliers so that the CC would not be held responsible for the defects. All the defects were to be rectified before handover to the hospital.

Another important aspect of the T&C process was the registration of the asset into the centralized management information system (CMIS) so that maintenance could take place. It is at this stage that the asset codes and identifications are established and entered into the CMIS to be used for future reference in the course of maintenance and operations.

In the T&C process, the CC acquired from the procurement contractor/ supplier all relevant documents, including O&M manuals, specifications, factory and site testing results and parameters, drawings, certifications, and historical information.

## 3.1.6. Asset Register

In the CA contract, two types of assets were generally categorized. Those more than RM500 in value were considered as assets, whilst those below RM500 in value were considered as inventory. Although this was the general rule, there were exceptions, as some assets below the RM500 range still required maintenance and thus were registered as assets. Inventory was a group of similar assets including tables and chairs.

Assets, according to the contract rules, were those items that required maintenance, had to be calibrated, or required statutory registration. Examples of assets below the RM500 range requiring maintenance are water heaters and small electrical appliances. Fire extinguishers, for example, are small-asset items needing constant maintenance, along with registration with the fire department, to ensure full functionality at all times.

Asset codes at the time of T&C were registered into the CMIS by the CCs, to be used for future reference in the administration of the CA contract.

## 3.1.7. Operation of Engineering Plants and Systems

The operation of the engineering plants and systems within the hospitals was a part of the main function and role of the CC in the contract for FEMS. The main goal was to ensure the efficient and optimal operation of all engineering plants and installations, whilst ensuring that all the systems in the hospitals functioned to the customers' satisfaction, did not compromise the safety of the occupants of the facility, and was comfortable for the patients and visitors.

Typically, the engineering plant systems and their components that are operated by the CC include the following:

a) **Ventilation and air conditioning** – chillers, cooling towers (including water treatment), water pumps, air-handling units, fan-coil units, and HEPA filters and humidifiers

b) **Centralized medical gases** – vacuum insulated evaporator (VIE) tanks, gas cylinder manifold system, pumps and compressors, and receiver tanks. The works carried out include verifying the receipt of gas supplies, inspecting and changing gas cylinders, and advising the hospital administration on the procurement of gases. The works to be carried out do not include the supply of medical gases

c) **Electrical supply** – main intake and distribution, substation, transformers, switchboards, stand-by generator(s), and centralized uninterruptible power supply system

d) **Water supply** – water storage tanks, piping, pumps, valves, and fittings

e) **Hot water supply** – boilers, clarifiers, piping system, valves, and pumps. The works do not include supply of fuel

f) **Steam supply** – boilers (including water treatment), steam header, chimney. The works do not include supply of fuels

g) **Vertical transportation** – lifts/elevators, dumbwaiters, and escalators

h) **Fire protection** – fire alarm panel, fire smoke/heat detector system, hose reel system, sprinkler system, wet riser and dry riser system, gas flooding system, automatic fire doors, and fire department communication links

i) **Sewerage system** – sewer line, sewerage treatment plant, and pumping station

j) **LPG, laboratory gas, and industrial gas** – gas manifold, piping, and directional safety valves. The works do not include supply of gases

k) **Centralized sterilization system**

l) **Pneumatic tube system** – control system blower, motor, diverter, receiver stations, and tubes

m) **PABX and telephone system** – main distribution frame (MDF) and sub-distribution frames (SDF)

n) **Building automatic system** – workstation (human interface division), supervisory (network/facility/floor) controls, direct digital controls, sensors, and actuators

To ensure efficient and optimal operations, the performance of the various systems was monitored by taking appropriate readings, and taking corrective action whenever the alarms were triggered. These readings and other observations made were recorded in proper log sheets. In addition, the CC recorded and monitored energy/utility usage and participated in the hospitals' energy conservation plans. Competent personal as required by regulations, such as chargemen and boilermen, were employed to handle the operations of the plants and systems.

## 3.1.8. Maintenance Management

Maintenance management was involved in the process of establishing a maintenance policy and planning, scheduling, and reviewing for the organization. Examples of the maintenance policy include outsourcing or carrying out maintenance in house; allowing equipment and systems to run until they fail or carrying out planned preventive maintenance; and maintaining parts of equipment by specialists, a trade group, or in house by a multiskilled task group.

Maintenance work is the prime function of facility engineering maintenance services. Based on best practices of maintenance management, maintenance activities are classified broadly as either planned or unplanned activities.

Planned maintenance consist of the maintenance activities that can be identified and defined well in advance of execution. This advance identification allows the maintenance work to be scheduled according to the service need, the availability of trained manpower, and the customer's needs. The schedules should be agreed on and approved by the customer, who could be the hospital. These activities include planned preventive maintenance, planned corrective maintenance, and routine inspections.

Planned preventive maintenance (PPM) is executed for all engineering systems, installations, and equipment in planned schedules and regular cycles, as recommended by the manufacturer and in accordance with good maintenance practices. PPM accounts for a major portion of the planned maintenance activities. Properly planned and executed preventive maintenance ensures optimal performance of the systems, thereby reducing the number of breakdowns and failures.

The CCs introduced predictive maintenance or conditioned-based monitoring in some of the engineering systems, such as using laser thermographs to detect overheating in motors and using the building automation system (BAS) to check on the health of chillers and air-conditioning systems in new hospitals. However, as there is no requirement in the concession agreement (CA), this practice is carried out on an ad hoc basis and sparsely.

For a PPM programme to be fully successful, the following things must be in place:

a) A team of dedicated, trained, hands-on, experienced, and competent workers to perform the PPM
b) Step-by-step procedures and schedules as recommended by manufacturer's guidelines and best industrial practices. These references should be incorporated in the organization's PPM procedure
c) A checklist of inspections from manufacturer's guidelines or industrial best practices
d) Keeping PPM schedules within certain windows/periods
e) Recording PPM schedules, breakdown record analyses, frequency and procedures, and maintenance costs (spare parts and labour cost)
f) A method of technical review to ensure that quality work is performed and that the PPM frequency and procedures are appropriate
g) A computerized maintenance management system (CMMS) in which the full technical and maintenance data are recorded and monitored.

Unplanned maintenance works include performing services requested by the users, performing breakdown repairs, and attending to failures or changes to the engineering plant/installation operations. Service requests include reports of faults observed by the user, and requests for specific services, such as redecoration of the wards or shifting of potted plants. Whereas the CC maintenance personnel can easily carry out some of the services requested, several of the service requests are for reimbursable works, which can only be implemented when the hospital authorities approve the budget for the said works. Breakdown repairs include breakdown maintenance works that are carried out when the user or the CC's maintenance personnel report the breakdown and/or fault to the help desk at the facility maintenance office. The breakdown repairs are carried out by appropriate and/or competent technical personnel so as to avoid abortive and repetitive works. Wherever warranted, upon completion of the breakdown repairs, the performance of the repaired equipment is checked and tested before returning the equipment to the user for use.

For both planned and unplanned maintenance, there is corrective maintenance to be carried out. Corrective maintenance is defined as the actions performed to restore an item to a specific condition after it fails. It includes routine corrective maintenance, breakdown maintenance, and emergency maintenance.

Scheduled corrective maintenance (SCM) is a subset of planned maintenance activity. It involves correcting deficiencies identified and detected during PPM or routine inspection (RI). Some of these deficiencies are repaired at the same time, whereas others are scheduled for other times because additional spare parts must be procured.

Inspection of the facility on a regular basis forms the backbone of all maintenance services. The activities consist of routine inspections, condition appraisal, inspection for code/regulation compliance, and ad hoc inspection. Routine inspections are scheduled inspections carried out at regular intervals by a group of technical personnel of various trades (an electrician, a plumber, and a carpenter, headed by experienced and qualified technicians). The purpose is to identify early defects and faults as a result of wear and tear. RI is carried out on buildings, mechanical systems, and electrical systems.

Condition appraisal is an audit function or process which is the means for producing the database for planning maintenance activities. It includes compiling the asset data and thoroughly assessing the current condition and functional performance of the buildings, engineering plants, systems, equipment, grounds, and utility services. A condition appraisal reports on the physical condition, operating condition, defects, shortcomings, problems, and safety of the asset or system. All data compiled are identified for rectification, corrective maintenance, upgrading, or replacement and are then presented in graphic format showing the frequency of breakdowns of assets over time, the cost of repairs of assets over time, the consumption of fuel of assets over time, etc. The condition appraisal might lead to exemption from penalization from technical requirements performance indicators (TRPI), beyond economic repair (BER) applications, and reimbursable work requests. An asset which is not repairable economically is recommended for BER certification.

## 3.1.9. Statutory Compliance

FEMS's facility managers for the healthcare facilities are responsible for complying with statutory regulations and for renewing and registering all necessary licenses and contractual obligations under their care.

The key laws and regulations which affect the services are mainly the following:

*Occupational Safety and Health Act (1994) (Act 514)*

This Act concerns safety and health in the workplace environment and requires the setting up of an Occupational Health and Safety committee, the implementation of a safety and health policy, the provision of protective clothing and devices for employees, safety inspections, and the management of risks and liabilities.

*Environmental Quality Act (1994)*

This Act relates to the protection and enhancement of the environment, and also includes the prevention, abatement, and control of pollution. Examples of regulations relevant to the hospital include the following:

- Environmental quality (sewerage and industrial effluent) regulations (1979)
- Environmental quality (clean air) regulations (1978)

*Factories and Machinery Act (1974)*

This Act governs the safe operation of select installations such as pressure vessels, boilers, sterilizers, elevators, and escalators. Apart from controlling the safety of these installations through annual inspection and licensing, this law also requires properly trained and certified personnel to operate the facilities under the purview of the Act. This includes the appointment of appropriate boilermen and/or competent steam engineers.

*Electrical Supply Act (1990), Regulations (1994),*
*and Electrical Inspectorate Act (1983)*

These laws require the appointment of competent personnel to operate, maintain, and inspect all electrical systems in the hospital facilities. The requirements include the following:

   i.   Competent electrical engineer to visit and inspect, at least once a month, the electrical installations not exceeding six hundred volts and switchgear not exceeding one hundred amps installations exceeding these limits require at least two visits a month.
   ii.  Certified chargeman of appropriate grade to operate and maintain high-tension and low-voltage switchgears and generators.
   iii. Certified wiremen to install and repair all internal electrical wiring and installations.
   iv.  Calibration of protection relays.

*Other Relevant Acts*

   •   Water Services Industrial Act (SPAN) (2006) for water and sewerage
   •   Fire Safety Act

Table 7, below, indicates some of the equipment and personnel associated with the particular licenses for renewals and registrations.

Table 7 **Equipment and personnel in association with a particular agency**

| Equipment/personnel | Agency | Renewal interval |
|---|---|---|
| Steam boiler | DOSH | Every 15 months |
| Lift and dumbwaiter | DOSH | Every 15 months |
| Compressed-air receivers | DOSH | Every 15 months |
| VIE tank | DOSH | Every 15 months |
| Sterilizers | DOSH | Every 15 months |
| Gas cylinders | DOSH | Every 5 years |

| Certificate of calibration (protective relay and devices) | JBEG | Biannually |
|---|---|---|
| Weighing scales | JST | Annually |
| Fire extinguishers | BOMBA | Annually |
| Sewerage treatment plant | DOE, SPAN | |
| Electrical chargemen/wiremen | JBEG | |
| Boilermen | DOSH | |
| Desludging contractor | SPAN | |

*Note:*    *Acronymns in the table can be referred to in the Glossary of Acronymns*

           *Agencies are government authorities responsible for regulating the various acts and discipline within their jurisdiction*

## 3.1.10. Beyond Economic Repair (BER)

Equipment for which the economic life has expired is considered for application for "beyond economic repair" (BER) certification by the CC. BER status for equipment is granted with justifications, which include obsolescence, safety considerations, no availability of spare parts or obsolescence of spare parts, high cost of spare parts, or the manufacturers or suppliers no longer being in operation. Before the equipment is declared as BER, the CC conducts a condition appraisal of the equipment. Final approval of BER status is granted by competent personnel from the hospital or the Ministry of Health (MOH).

## 3.2. Biomedical Engineering Maintenance Services (BEMS)

### 3.2.1. General

The BEMS covers maintenance of all diagnostic, therapeutic, laboratory, and other associated and allied equipment used for the hospital services. BEMS involves a comprehensive maintenance programme implemented for all biomedical equipment in the inventory list of the hospital under the CA. Maintenance practices are in accordance with related legislation, such as OSHA (1994).

## 3.2.2. Scope of Works

The scope of works for BEMS is as follows:

a) To carry out a comprehensive programme of planned and scheduled maintenance for all medical and laboratory equipment
b) To provide effective and responsive repair on all medical equipment and to provide on-call and emergency services
c) To carry out acceptance testing as well as to assess safety and performance characteristics of all incoming medical equipment
d) To provide mechanisms to avoid failure or breakdown during diagnosis or therapy
e) To carry out all works necessary to guarantee equipment uptime
f) To implement the hospital's engineering quality assurance programme
g) To establish a computerized documentation system which includes a record of equipment control
h) To provide quarterly reports on maintenance activities to the MOH and hospital administration
i) To notify departments of warranty expirations
j) To dispose of/remove unwanted medical equipment
k) To provide procedures for dealing with hazardous matter and handling contaminated equipment
l) To train users on the daily maintenance procedures
m) To maintain a stock of genuine spare parts
n) To establish a library of user and service manuals

## 3.2.3. Objectives of BEMS

The objectives of BEMS are to:

- Ensure performance of the medical equipment in terms of quality, safety, efficiency, and availability
- Reduce cost of maintenance
- Minimize risk to patients
- Comply with regulatory requirements.

## 3.2.4. Classification of BEMS equipment

BEMS equipment is classified into the following categories:

- Diagnostic
- Therapeutic
- Laboratory

Groupings include equipment for patient support, life support, and critical care. Diagnostic medical equipment includes equipment for imaging, such as X-ray machines, ECGs, EEGs, oximeters, blood gas analysers, etc. Therapeutic medical equipment includes haemodialysis machines, infusion devices, defibrillators, phototherapy, radiotherapy, ventilators, etc. Laboratory equipment includes clinical chemical analysers, spectrophotometers, pH meters, centrifuges, glucose analysers, microscopes, etc.

## 3.2.5. Four Elements of Patient Care

The four elements of patient care are as follows:

a) Diagnosis and monitoring
b) Information collection and clinical information system
c) Interpretation
d) Therapy

## 3.2.6. Life Cycle of Medical Equipment

The life cycle of medical equipment is similar to the life cycle of FEMS equipment, as shown in Figure 7. The difference is in the emphasis at each stage of the life cycle. The testing, commissioning, and maintenance of medical equipment is important, as patient care is dependent on the accuracy and proper functioning of the equipment. Any failure at these stages could lead to unwarranted loss of life. Thus, competent technical personnel must be employed for this task.

## 3.2.7. Maintenance of Biomedical Engineering Equipment

In the maintenance of biomedical engineering equipment, many aspects of the maintenance regime is similar to that of facilities engineering maintenance equipment like PPM, unplanned maintenance, routine inspection (RI), and scheduled corrective maintenance (SCM). However, there are different variations, emphases, and approaches for maintaining biomedical equipment because it is critical for life support and patient care. For instance, the electrical safety standards and requirements are different for biomedical equipment than they are for ordinary facilities equipment such as an air conditioner. Safety tests are an important component of maintaining BEMS equipment, as non-compliance can lead to injuries or the death of a patient.

The core activities in biomedical engineering maintenance involve PPM, corrective maintenance (CM), acceptance testing, and decommissioning of medical equipment.

PPM is scheduled maintenance carried out on a regular basis, as determined by the CC and the hospital and as recorded in the hospital-specific implementation plan (HSIP). A comprehensive plan to carry out PPM includes checklists as per the TRPI; the manufacturer's PPM or the hospital engineering planned preventive maintenance (HEPPM), with the manufacturer excerpts attached and the reference quoted from service manuals; the frequency of PPM; and the type of PPM (whether major or minor). In addition to the CC, vendors also carry out PPM on their behalf with advance notice. During the course of carrying out the PPM, some potential faults might be identified; hence, the user should be informed and a date should be set to perform the scheduled corrective maintenance. The scheduled maintenance for biomedical equipment that uses radiation includes an annual assessment of quality assurance.

Unscheduled maintenance (UM) provides effective and responsive repair of all broken-down equipment. UM includes corrective maintenance. It is to be completed on a best-effort basis to ensure the continuation of service. Uptime targets for equipment are ensured through the provision of a sufficient stock of spare parts, the provision of loaner equipment, and the provision of alternative services where applicable. UM seeks to rectify defects with due diligence. All repair works to BEMS equipment should be completed with performance and electrical safety tests. Parts and fast-moving items should be stocked as necessary in order to facilitate and hasten maintenance activity.

Acceptance testing is qualitative and quantitative testing carried out on biomedical equipment to ensure its safety and performance and to ascertain that it is in accordance with the manufacturer's specifications, purchase agreements, and statutory requirements. The objective of acceptance testing is to establish the procedure for carrying out acceptance testing for all new medical equipment before it is placed into clinical service. Procedures for performing acceptance testing of biomedical equipment include the following:

- The client informs the CC in advance of the arrival of new biomedical equipment.
- The user ensures that the correct items are delivered in good condition based on the purchase document.
- The user, the vendor, and the CC witness acceptance testing.
- The CC ensures that appropriate performance tests using a dedicated test tool/instrument/analyser are carried out by the vendor.
- Once the equipment is accepted, the CC carries out safety testing and issues an inspection certificate.
- The CC tags the assets and registers the equipment in the management information system (MIS).
- The users receive a copy of the results of the acceptance test.
- Equipment which fails the test or which has no complete manuals and is subsequently not accepted is noted and is subject to acceptance testing again upon rectification of the problem.
- If rectifications to the biomedical equipment are required, they should comply with the manufacturer's recommendations.
- The warranty period is initiated by the CC and recorded in the MIS.

The decommissioning of medical equipment is done by way of the BER process. A building, plant, or piece of equipment is recommended for BER status when it becomes obsolete, when repair expenses exceed the depreciated value, when the item is no longer reliable, when it doesn't conform to any statutory requirement, or when it must be transferred out of the hospital and moved to a lesser hospital. Obsolescence is determined when there is a new model of the same type of equipment featuring a design change and resulting in better efficiency and increased capacity; then there is increased capacity because of expanded operations or less labour availability; when the existing concept for the service provided by the equipment is not acceptable to the MOH; when new safety requirements render the equipment unsafe; when genuine or approved equivalent spare parts are no longer available; and when third-party service agents are not available and the equipment cannot be repaired in house. Unreliability is determined when it is declared uneconomical for the equipment to regain the proper level of reliability and when it is no longer dependable for completing the job in the time available.

## 3.3. Cleansing Services (CLS)

### 3.3.1. General

Healthcare facilities face mounting pressures not only to provide a physically safe environment which is clean and pleasant but also to protect the patients, visitors, and staff from the hazards of infection and disease. Cleanliness in any building complex is absolutely essential to the physical health and well-being of the building occupants. In hospitals, more often than not, the level and quality of patient care is perceived to be equal to the level of cleanliness of the hospital premises and the quality of the hospital environment. Generally, hospitals require stringent levels of quality, particularly in specialized patient-care areas. The level of cleanliness affects the control of nosocomial infections (hospital-acquired infections). Outbreaks of nosocomial infections at hospitals are attributed to the lack of cleanliness; hence the need to institute good housekeeping and cleaning practices.

To adequately address these concerns, the Malaysian MOH privatized the cleansing services (CLS) of all government hospitals and selected institutions, along with four other hospital support services, ascribing the CLS to three concession companies on 1st January 1997 for a fifteen-year contract period.

### 3.3.2. Objectives of CLS

The overall objectives of the cleansing services (CLS) are to standardize procedures and schedules for all contract hospitals and to create an impressive hygienic and clean hospital image.

The objectives of CLS for the concession companies are to provide and manage the CLS effectively and efficiently for the various user locations within the compound of the contract hospital, in accordance to the TRPI, the MAP, and the HSIP. The services also include the usage of only MOH-approved chemicals, the supply of associated consumables, and the supply of receptacles and black plastic bags for general waste.

### 3.3.3. Scope of Works

The scope of works for CLS to be performed by the contractor are as follows:

a) The methods and procedures of cleansing, including the tools and equipment used for cleansing, are to meet the required standard of hygiene, and cleansing is to be performed at an agreed frequency without causing any interference in the hospital's daily functioning.
b) There is to be a provision of adequate consumables and dispensers for all user locations.
c) General waste is to be collected at the point of generation and then transported to a central storage facility.
d) Waste collection is to follow an agreed schedule and to be done via designated routes and using a suitable collection device for such purpose.
e) A sufficient number of black plastic bags that meet the standards for general waste is to be provided.
f) Suitable and adequate containers are to be close to the source of generation of general waste.
g) A dedicated storage container for general waste is to be designed, constructed, operated, and maintained as per MOH stipulations.
h) Joint inspections with MOH personnel are to be carried out on an agreed schedule.

### 3.3.4. Coverage of Service

The coverage of the cleaning service includes the following areas:

a) Wards, clinics, departments, and other areas in the hospital, such as lobbies, railings, corridors, staircase, and toilets, as well as specialized area(s) identified by the hospital

b) Common areas, including areas within the hospital compound that are rented out to private sectors
c) Hospital kitchen, including its food preparation areas
d) Public areas of the hospital canteen

## 3.3.5. Purpose of Cleaning

The purpose of cleaning services in the hospitals is to do the following things:

a) Control the accumulation of dust and dirt
b) Control the spread of disease
c) Promote health, hygiene, and safety
d) Promote a clean and healthy environment
e) Add aesthetic value to the property
f) Provide higher real estate returns (yields or ROI)

## 3.3.6. Cleaning Activities

Cleaning activities in hospitals include the following:

a) Cleaning of floors using wet and dry mops and/or vacuums, including spot cleaning and removal of spillage; under no circumstances should brooms be used
b) Vacuuming of carpeted floors daily, and shampooing of carpeted floors once every month
c) Buffing and burnishing of vinyl, terrazzo, marble, granite, and other polishable floors at least once a week, or as required, using approved chemicals
d) Stripping and polishing of vinyl, terrazzo, and other polishable floors which are required to be polished, at least once every three months, using appropriate chemicals
e) Scrubbing and washing of floors of all types of tiled and cement-rendered surface
f) Dusting of walls, ceilings, doors/windows, furniture, and fixtures regularly
g) Damp wiping and spot cleaning of all walls, columns, windows, door frames, window frames, partitions, and fixed glass panels

h) Damp wiping of all furniture and fixtures, such as fans, covers to light fittings, air-conditioning grilles/outlets, exposed pipework, exterior of cabinets, refrigerators, and other installed equipment, shelves, and framed pictures/posters/noticeboards

i) Damp wiping or washing, and sanitizing, of all counters and worktops, sinks, washbasins, drinking fountains, water coolers, patient beds, bedside lockers, wheelchairs, patient transport trolleys/stretcher carts, and telephone handsets

j) Rearranging displaced furniture and equipment after completing cleaning tasks

k) Supplying and replenishing consumables such as liquid hand soap, paper hand towels, and toilet paper rolls, including appropriate dispensers/holders and deodorizers

## 3.3.7. Cleaning Equipment

Cleaning equipment used for cleansing includes the following:

- Dry mop – different colour mops have different purposes
- Wet mop – round, Kentucky
- Mop press
- Buckets – single and double
- Edging tools
- Floor squeegee
- Abrasive pads
- Service trolley
- Suctions – cylindrical
- Backpack suction cleaner
- Canister vacuum cleaner
- Upright vacuum cleaner
- Carpet extraction machine – injection and vacuum
- Powder cleaning machine
- Blower
- Scrubber and polisher
- High-pressure cleaner – hot/cold water jet
- Industrial sweeping machine

## 3.3.8. Cleaning Chemicals

Chemicals used in cleaning are mainly detergents, acids, and disinfectants, as water alone is not able to clean stubborn stains. Some of the chemicals used are as listed below. All chemicals used for cleaning need to be approved by the hospital and the Ministry of Health.

Table 8  **pH values**

| Description | pH level | Function |
|---|---|---|
| Neutral | 7 | Mild and routine cleaning (i.e. general cleaning) |
| Acidic | 1 to 6 | Harsh chemical for removing stains that occur naturally |
| Alkaline | 8 to 14 | Slightly stronger detergent for removing man-made stains |

Table 9  **Disinfectants**

| Level | Grade | Type |
|---|---|---|
| Low | Non-hospital grade | • NaOCl <br> • Lysol |
| Intermediate | Hospital grade | • NaDCC <br> • Phenol <br> • Chlorhexidine gluconate <br> • Povidone iodine |
| High | Hospital grade (CSSD) | • Glutaraldehyde <br> • Ethylene oxide |

# 3.4. Linen Laundry Services (LLS)

## 3.4.1. General

In the past, before the privatization of hospital support services, the supply of clean linen, the collection and processing of the soiled linen, and the management of laundry services were very much the responsibility of the hospitals. With the privatization, LLS was contracted to three companies. The scope of work for these companies includes a proper programme for the delivery of adequate clean linen to the contract hospitals and for the removal of soil linen, which is to be processed at centralized laundry facilities.

## 3.4.2. Scope of Service

The scope of service for linen is as follows:

1.  The contractor is to deliver clean linen to all user locations according to the schedules, frequency, and routes agreed by the user.
2.  The contractor is to ensure that the quality of clean linen delivered meets the requirement of each user location, in terms of the linen type, size, and quantity agreed by each user department/ward and documented in the HSIP.
3.  A collection of soiled linen is to be made daily or as required and agreed by the user locations and documented in the HSIP at each contract hospital. Users are to dispose of soiled linen by placing it in the appropriate-colour soiled-linen bag located in designated areas – usually the dirty-linen room.
4.  The user is to ensure that the heavily soiled and infected linen with a high moisture content is placed into an alginate bag before being disposed of in the red bag, which is lined.
5.  The contractor is to use a designated trolley for the collection of soiled linen, which has a blue cover sheet. The soiled-linen bags, upon collection from the user locations, are to be tied, tagged to identify their origin, and removed from the user location.
6.  The contractor, upon arriving at the soiled-linen sorting area, is to weigh the soiled linen in the presence of the hospital representative, record the weight, and sign the Soiled Linen Weight Record form.
7.  The bag holders at the user location are to be washed and sanitized on a weekly basis and whenever necessary.
8.  To ensure proper laundry operations, all laundry equipment at the central plant is to be maintained in compliance with the stipulated regulations and standards.
9.  All soiled linen is to be processed using the appropriate linen wash formula, which should include validated thermal disinfection. Appropriate tests should be carried out on processed water to ensure

that the pH value of the finished clean linen is neutral and does not pose a skin-irritation problem to the patients.

10. The contractor is to ensure that all wash process parameters, and in particular the thermal disinfection temperature and time requirements, are checked and validated for each washer used on a monthly basis. The contractor is to maintain records of these validations and to make them available for MOH/hospital/SIHAT inspection at any time.

11. The linen should be washed, thermally disinfected, and finished according to the United Kingdom Fabric Care Research Association (FCRA) Handbook or approved equivalent standards. The tests include those for whiteness, chemical residue, tensile strength, and bacteria count to ensure clean linen and an acceptable laundering process.

### 3.4.3. Definition

Linen laundry service is defined as the delivery of adequate clean linen to the contract hospitals and the removal of soiled linen, which is to be processed at centralized laundry facilities.

### 3.4.4. Quality of Linen

The contractor is to ensure that the quality of clean linen delivered meets the requirement of each user location, in terms of both linen type and size. However, the contractor needs to comply with the minimum quantity, as follows:

a) Wards – the shelf stock level should be at least two par levels for bed and patient linen, and one par level for other ward linen. The first par level should be based on total bed strength, and the second par level should be based on the daily bed occupancy rate at the ward. In addition, the contractor should maintain at least one par level for bed and patient linen at the clean linen store at the contract hospital. One par level at the ward is the average quantity required per day for each linen item.

b) Central Sterile Supply Department (CSSD) – there should be at least three shelf par levels. The three par levels required are (1) for linen prior to the sterilization process, (2) for linen in the process, and (3) for linen after processing. In addition to this, two par levels should be made available for linen to be distributed to the user locations.

c) Other areas, such as X-ray, physiotherapy, clinics, etc. – the shelf stock quantities for patient-related linen should be maintained at one par level, with an additional par level maintained at the linen store. Non-patient-related linen should be maintained at one par level.

All clean linen should be supplied and delivered to the user locations daily using a top-up system. The contractor's linen delivery personnel should stack up the clean linen properly in the user's linen store to ensure good stock rotation.

Clean linen items that are considered unusable or below quality standards should be rejected by the user. The user should place the rejected linen items into the designated white bag complete with yellow tag for collection. The contractor should replace the rejected linen on a like-for-like basis and deliver the fresh linen to the user location concerned within twenty-four hours.

## 3.5. Clinical Waste Management Services (CWMS)

### 3.5.1. General

It is known that healthcare facilities generate waste that is hazardous and poses a health risk to healthcare workers and patients. Thus, careful handling of waste within a healthcare facility is essential.

Up until the 1980s, Malaysia had no proper system for the management of medical and clinical waste. This situation was made worse by the emergence of AIDS and other communicable diseases, and public fear. Despite the lack of evidence that human immunodeficiency virus could be transmitted by way of hospital waste, the public perception was that clinical waste transmitted disease. Compounding this problem were environmental pollution concerns and the high cost of waste disposal. All of these factors contributed to the challenge that healthcare facilities face to mitigate the risks associated with clinical waste whilst addressing public perceptions of the risks.

To address these issues, the MOH, in collaboration with the Department of Environment (DOE), took the initiative to include clinical waste in the category of scheduled waste, which is defined in the Environmental Quality (Scheduled Wastes) Regulations (1989) under the Environmental Quality Act. In 1993, clinical waste management was adopted by the MOH, and policies, guidelines, and action plans for clinical waste management were developed. The basic components required for the effective management of clinical waste are generation, segregation, storage, collection, transportation, and disposal. For the effective management of clinical waste for MOH hospitals, three concession companies were appointed in 1997 to undertake this task. These MOH hospitals throughout the country met international standards for clinical waste management.

### 3.5.2. Definition of Clinical Waste

Clinical waste[6] is mainly defined as follows:

i.   Any waste which consists wholly or partly of human or animal tissue, blood or other bodily fluids, excretions, drugs or other pharmaceutical products, swabs or dressings, syringes, and needles or other sharp instruments – any waste which, unless rendered safe, might prove hazardous to any person coming into contact with it

ii.  Any other waste arising from medical, nursing, dental, veterinary, pharmaceutical, or similar practice, investigation, treatment, care, teaching, or research, or the collection of blood for transfusion, being waste which might cause infection to any person coming into contact with it.

### 3.5.3. Scope of Service

The scope of service for CWMS by the concession companies includes the following:

a)   Supply of suitable receptacles for the storage of clinical waste at the user locations; these include yellow/blue bags, bag holders, clinical waste bins, and sharps containers, all of which have to meet MOH specifications and requirements

---

[6]   Source: Health Regulations Northern Ireland

b) Collection of segregated clinical waste (CW) at dedicated collection trolleys according to a pre-agreed schedule and route
c) Storage of CW at dedicated storage facilities prior to transportation
d) Transportation of CW using licensed and dedicated vehicles from the contract hospitals to a licensed CW incinerator
e) Incineration of CW at licensed dedicated CW incinerators, which must comply with the licensing conditions, including the provision of effective pollution control systems and disposal of ash to licensed scheduled waste disposal facilities licensed by the Department of Environment (DOE)
f) Documentation, and compliance with all statutory requirements

### 3.5.4. Coverage of Service

The coverage of the service includes the following user locations:

a) Medical areas and departments, including specialized areas such as operating theatres and delivery rooms
b) Allied polyclinics/satellite clinics under the administration of the contract hospital
c) Other MOH facilities such as health centres, clinics, etc., as and when requested. However, such MOH facility shall be responsible for collection and transportation to the nearest contract hospital.

### 3.5.5. Classification of Clinical Waste

There are various types of waste generated in a hospital, but only 10 per cent to 15 per cent of waste generated in hospitals is potentially infectious. Therefore, proper classification of waste is essential for a cost-effective and successful implementation of the clinical waste management service. Hazardous waste is classified as different types according to the source, the risk, and the factors associated with its handling, storage, transport, and ultimate disposal. The types of waste include the following:

a) Infectious healthcare waste
b) Anatomical and pathological waste
c) Sharps

d) Pharmaceutical and chemical waste
e) Radioactive waste

Under the Environmental Quality (Schedule Waste) Regulation (1989), all of the types of waste in the list above are classified as scheduled waste and are found in the hospital environment.

Infectious waste is waste suspected to contain pathogens (bacteria, viruses, parasites, or fungi) in sufficient concentration or quantity to cause disease in susceptible hosts. This category includes the following:

- Cultures and stocks of infectious agents from laboratory work
- Waste from surgeries or autopsies on patients who have an infectious disease
- Waste from infected patients in an isolation ward
- Waste that had been in contact with infected patients undergoing haemodialysis
- Infected animals from laboratories
- Any other instruments or materials that had been in contact with infected persons or animals
- Cultures and stocks of highly infectious agents
- Waste from autopsies and animal bodies

Anatomical or pathological waste consists of tissues, organ, body parts, human foetuses, animal carcasses, blood, and body fluids. This category is considered to be a subcategory of infectious waste.

Sharps are items that can cause cuts or puncture wounds. Needles, hypodermic needles, scalpels and other blades, knives, infusion sets, saws, broken glass, and nails are considered to be highly hazardous healthcare waste.

## 3.5.6. Cradle-to-Grave Concept of Clinical Waste Management

The cradle-to-grave concept best describes the process of managing clinical waste, which is the period between the source of waste generation and the disposal of the clinical waste. The stages of clinical waste disposal are generation, segregation, collection, storage, transportation, and disposal.

*Generation*

The source of generation could be any of the following areas on the hospital premises:

i. Medical areas and departments, including specialized areas such as operating theatres and delivery rooms

ii. Allied polyclinics/satellite clinics under the administration of the contract hospital

iii. Other MOH facilities such as health centres, clinics, etc., outside the hospital.

*Segregation*

Segregation is the key to effective clinical waste management. It should be carried out as close as possible to the point of generation and should not involve dangerous secondary sorting. The segregation system should be uniformly applied throughout the whole country of Malaysia. Common system of labelling and packaging should be adopted. In MOH, the colour-coding system for waste bins and bags is as follows:

- Black – general waste
- Yellow – clinical waste
- Light blue – waste requiring immediate disinfection

*Collection and Internal Transportation*

The collection of clinical waste should be performed at least once a day, and the waste should not be stored for more than 48 hours. A 660-litre wheeled bin is used by porters to transport the clinical waste bags to the temporary store, where they are re-stored in 15-kg wheeled bins. Routes for internal transportation are carefully planned and scheduled to minimize spillage and contamination.

Porters commence their duty by entering every ward or clinic to collect the clinical waste in pedal bins and sharps containers. The porters should be properly trained to handle medical waste and should wear suitable personal protective equipment, including a face mask, an apron, gloves, and shoes. After collection, the porters gather all yellow bags and sharps containers in one storeroom on the same level of the building. These are then loaded into the 660-litre wheeled bins for delivery to the temporary store in the hospital.

*Temporary Storage*

The purpose of having temporary storage when managing clinical waste is to provide a place where the waste can be stored temporarily, safely, and easily for inspection. The temporary storage area needs to have good air circulation and ventilation. For proper control, clinical waste is to be stored in refrigerated storage facilities with the temperature maintained at four to six degrees Celsius to prevent bacteria from breeding and to prevent odour problem before disposal. Wherever possible, all clinical waste should be removed from this temporary store within a day. This is to ensure that the waste does not deteriorate rapidly and become even more hazardous. The guidelines for the temporary storage facility include three days for collection and a minimum of two days' storage.

*External Transportation*

Special containers and vehicles are to be used in the transportation of clinical waste, with full documentation of the clinical waste from generation point to disposal facility. Well-designed vehicles meeting specific criteria are used for external transportation. The inner space of the vehicle storage is lined with stainless steel and aluminium to provide a smooth surface for cleaning purposes. The vehicle must not be used for other purposes. Drivers of these vehicles are required to adhere to strict operational requirements for the delivery of the clinical waste to the incineration plants. If there is to be any delay in delivery, the driver is to inform his or her superior office. Drivers are prohibited from leaving the vehicle under any circumstances during transportation. The routes chosen for the transportation should avoid highly populated residential areas, bodies of water, and sensitive areas.

*Disposal*

Incineration has been adopted as the best option for the disposal of clinical waste. However, contingency plans needed to be established in the event of incinerator failure. Most modern clinical waste incinerators operate on controlled air and use two chambers. The primary chamber operates with a restricted air flow at 1600 to 1800 degrees Fahrenheit. The waste is pyrolysed and the volatiles moved up to a secondary chamber. Ash generated moves through and exits the primary chamber by use of hydraulic rams or other feed devices.

Incineration enables the combustion of waste in a controlled manner in order to destroy or transform the waste into less hazardous waste. It allows for detoxification, especially for combustible carcinogens, pathogen-contaminated material, toxic organ compounds, or biologically active material that would affect sewerage treatment plants.

*Documentation*

The DOE regulations require an inventory be kept and a consignment note system to be used for the transport of waste from the hospital to an approved disposal facility. The consignment note or form is designed to record the name of the hospital, name and signature of the officer, name of the driver(s), the vehicle(s) used, etc.

The steps of the procedure for using the consignment note at the hospital level are as follows:

i. Clinical waste weight is to be calculated and recorded in a consignment note. This information needs to be filled in on seven copies, with a copy kept by the hospital, a copy sent to the MOH, a copy sent to the DOE, and the balance (four copies) taken by the driver to the incinerator.

ii. At the incinerator, information about the consignment is written on the consignment note, which is signed by the incinerator operator. The operator then returns a copy to the driver.

iii. After all the waste is disposed of, the operator sends a copy of the consignment note to the hospital and sends a copy to the DOE. The incinerator operator keeps a copy.

## 3.5.7. Bags and Sharps Containers

*Bags*

Clinical waste is collected and contained in bags before being transported and disposed of. Waste is segregated according to its hazardous nature: yellow bags for clinical waste, light blue bags for waste requiring immediate disinfection, and black bags for general waste.

The plastic bags must fulfil the standard in BS 6642: 1985: Specification for Disposable Plastic Bags from Polyethylene Material. The thickness of the plastic bag must be at least G225 (55 microns) for lower-density waste and at least G100 (25 microns) for higher-density waste. Yellow plastic bags are available in 5L, 30L, and 100L sizes.

The CC is to ensure that a sufficient supply of bags is made available at each user location. Bags should be filled only three quarters to allow for easy sealing with plastic bands or tie-ups and subsequent transportation. Full bags are loaded into wheeled bins and are taken to a temporary storage area in the hospital for transportation to an incineration plant. The bags and wheeled bins are incinerated together with the waste at the incinerators. For identification, all wheeled containers are marked with the biohazard logo.

*Sharps Containers*

Sharps containers are provided in various sizes, e.g. 2.5L, 5L, 10L, and 20L containers (BS 7320). The sharps containers must meet the following specifications:

- The containers must have handles.
- The containers must be of high durability, puncture-proof, and leakproof, even if upside down.
- The containers must be able to be removed without the threat of the waste dislodging and spilling.
- The container's opening needs to be able to close tightly and safely when the waste has reached the container's three-quarters-full mark.
- The container's opening needs to close tightly during transportation.
- The container's material must be able to burn in the incinerator.

## 3.5.8. Legal Compliance

At the time of the contract, the laws and regulations governing the control of clinical waste in Malaysia were as follows:

a) DOE requirements – Environment Quality (Schedule Wastes) Regulation (1989) under Environmental Quality Act (1974) (Act 127)
b) MOH requirements – Prevention and Control of Infectious Diseases Act (1988) (Act 342)
c) Atomic Energy Licensing Act (1984) for radioactive waste

# Chapter 4

# The Monitoring Consultant – SIHAT

## General

*Sistem Hospital Awasan Taraf Sdn Bhd*, or SIHAT, was the consultant appointed by the Ministry of Health (MOH) to assist in the monitoring and supervision of the concession companies carrying out the provision of hospital support services (HSS) to the hospitals and health institutions during the period of the project. SIHAT performed numerous roles, including performance monitoring and supervising the concession companies, and consulting with and advising the contract hospitals. SIHAT was appointed as the monitoring consultant in 27 October 1997 for a contract period of five years, from 1997 to 2002. Thereafter, there was extension of the contract on monitoring, from October 2002 to February 2006. A new agreement was implemented from March 2006 to February 2011. Presently, SIHAT still plays an important consultancy role for the MOH.

## 4.1. Scope of Service

The scope of services provided by SIHAT covered two major areas, namely monitoring and consulting. Within each of these services was a subdivision of services, which are listed below.

### 4.1.1. Monitoring Services

*Monitor and Report on the Works, Supplies, and Services Provided by the Contractors*

This involved carrying out scheduled visits to all contract hospitals. The actual number of scheduled visits for each month was provided to the respective hospital and agreed to. The tasks performed at each hospital consisted of the following:

- Verifying the hospital-specific implementation plan (HSIP) upon each revision made by the contractor yearly and prior to approval by the hospital director.
- Conducting regular inspections at user locations and contractors' facilities on a sampling basis using appropriate field inspection checklists created by SIHAT, based on an agreed yearly and monthly hospital inspection plan. Contractors' on-site facilities that were within the scope of the contract included facilities such as incinerator, laundry plant, clinical waste store, linen store, FEMS workshop, BEMS workshop, general waste stores, and dedicated vehicles for clinical waste, linen, and stores (to ensure that only approved materials, chemicals, and equipment were being used by the contractors).
- Inspecting and verifying reports and records in the centralized management information system (CMIS) at each contract hospital using the appropriate field inspection checklist created by SIHAT. This was to ensure the functionality of the designated CMIS terminal at each contract hospital, and the completeness, accuracy, and correctness of the reports and records from CMIS based on hard-copy records on a sampling basis, at least once a month.
- Annually inspecting all assets (FEMS and BEMS) at each contract hospital to ensure that data and information were captured completely and correctly in the CMIS based on the data stipulated by the government's standard procedure for inventory and asset listing. Mandatory data included the identity of the contract hospital, the department and location, and a description of the asset, such as asset type, asset category code, asset tag/label number, manufacturer, model, serial number, chassis number and/or registration number, purchase cost, and purchase date. Additional information like records of variation status, maintenance history, and uptime in the CMIS were verified to be correct and complete.
- Monitoring and reporting on the performance of the regional clinical waste (CW) incinerators and laundry plants utilized by the contractors. This was to ensure proper performance, including compliance with the service requirements and statutory regulations.

- Carrying out a detailed, comprehensive objective assessment of the hospital support services at selected contract hospitals, which included assessing the essential elements such as the adequacy of any written implementation plans, policies, and operating procedures; the user training programme; and the local-level mechanism for the monitoring and evaluation of the quality of services provided by the contractor. The objectives of the objective assessment were to assess whether the HSS were being managed effectively, based on the observations made at the selected contract hospitals; to assess the initiatives and improvements made by the contract hospitals/contractors; to develop the database to benchmark contractors' performance, which would be used for future assessment of the HSS; and to provide recommendations for improvements to be made by the contract hospitals, consulting companies, and contractors concerned.
- Issuing non-conformance reports (NCRs) to the contractors for any non-conforming and non-compliant services/procedures or facilities, and thereafter monitoring the closure of the NCRs issued.
- Documenting, to show for historical and annual comparison purposes, the progressive improvement achieved in the HSS by the contractors by compiling relevant data, documents, and photographic evidence to show the progressive improvements, the non-conformance, and the benefits provided by the contractors, in addition to their contractual obligations, and to coordinate with the contractors on the production of appropriate audiovisual presentations to illustrate the progressive improvements.
- Organizing and/or meeting with the contractors on related specific issues.
- Preparing and submitting the following reports: monthly summary reports of scheduled visits to MOH; hospital monthly reports (HMRs) to contract hospitals by the last working day of the month capturing all findings and observations made during the month; semi-annual summary reports of contractors to MOH; contractors' reports and records in CMIS; semi-annual summary reports to MOH on the status of asset data in the CMIS; reports on the inspection of regional incinerators/laundries to MOH; reports on objective assessment at selected hospitals to MOH; and an annual comparison report to MOH for the five HSS.

*Monitor and Report on Compliance with Statutory Requirements*

This aspect of the SIHAT's scope of works involved the inspection of records at the contract hospitals, including verification of reports of irradiation apparatuses submitted by the contractors and the quality checks of selected irradiation apparatuses at the contract hospitals. The objectives were as follows:

i.  To inspect records and certification of personnel/equipment/plant/ installation that required compliance with appropriate statutory legislation at the contract hospitals, ensuring that all items inspected and personnel data checked had been captured correctly in the CMIS as follows:

    -   To identify the systems and assets that require the certification of the Department of Occupational Safety and Health (DOSH), as follows:
        •   Fired pressure vessels, including steam boilers, water boilers, and steam generators for autoclaves
        •   Unfired pressure vessels, including steam headers, hot water clarifiers, water softeners, deaerators, autoclaves, steam rice cookers, steam kettles, air compressors, air receiver tanks (medical or non-medical), vacuum receiver tanks, LPG bulk storage tanks, LPG oil separators, and vacuum insulated evaporator (VIE) tanks for liquid oxygen storage
        •   Hoisting equipment, including lifts, escalators, paternosters, dumbwaiters and hoists

    -   To identify fire detection and protection systems, and portable fire extinguishers, which require certification by the Fire Services Department
    -   To identify a hospital's weighing scales in the kitchen and stores, which require certification by the Department of Weights and Measures
    -   To identify substations, the main incoming panel, protective relays and devices, the transformer, standby generator sets, LPG installations, and gas manifolds, which require registration with and/or certification by the Energy Commission

- To ensure sewage treatment plant maintenance, which requires the contractor to be registered with the Sewerage Department
- To ensure effluent quality, which is regulated by the Department of Environment
- To identify contractor-owned facilities and assets, including assets that must comply with statutory regulations, such as calibration of weighing scales used for clinical waste and clean/soiled linen, license/certificate of fitness for incinerators and laundry plant (steam roller ironer or calendar, garment presses, steam boilers), and commercial vehicle licenses/RTD registration/PUSPAKOM inspection of vehicles used for transportation of clinical waste and linen
- To identify contractors' personnel – electrical chargemen, steam boilermen, visiting engineers (electrical/steam), electrical wiremen, electrical contractors for calibration of protective relays and devices, lift-competent persons, Class H consultants/maintenance personnel for radiological equipment, and drivers of vehicles transporting clinical waste and linens
- To issue, and to monitor the closure of, NCRs for all cases of non-compliance (non-valid or expired certification)
- To report to the contract hospital concerned any equipment/plant/installation which did not have valid initial certification
- To investigate cases of prolonged non-compliance on the part of the contractor and to submit reports with recommendations to the MOH/contract hospitals
- To coordinate and/or attend meetings with the contractors on related specific issues, as and when requested or consented to by MOH/contract hospitals

ii. To verify the reports and records submitted by contractors declaring that the maintenance of all irradiating apparatuses, all film processors, and the integrity of the X-ray room protection were in compliance with the requirements of the Atomic Energy Licensing Act (1984) and MS 838

iii. To carry out quality checks (QC) on randomly selected irradiation apparatuses, film processors, and radiation protection in X-ray rooms at contract hospitals to validate that the QC tests done by the contractors were in compliance with the Atomic Energy Act and MS 838, as follows:

   a.   QC test up to a ceiling of *x* number of irradiating apparatuses per annum, including the various types of irradiating apparatuses
   b.   QC test on up to ceiling of *x* number of film processors per annum
   c.   Measurements on the integrity of the X-ray room's protection up to a ceiling of *x* number of X-ray rooms per annum

iv.   To prepare and submit the following reports:

   a.   An update of the status of compliance with statutory legislations, to be reported in the monthly reports to the contract hospitals
   b.   A quarterly status report on the contractors' compliance with the Atomic Energy Licensing Act (1984) and MS 838, sent to MOH
   c.   Reports on the random QC tests on irradiating apparatuses, film processors, and darkrooms, sent to the contract hospital concerned and MOH
   d.   A semi-annual summary report on the status of compliance with relevant statutory legislations, sent to MOH
   e.   Investigation reports on cases of prolonged non-compliance, sent to MOH and the contract hospital concerned, as and when deemed necessary.

*Monitor and Report on the Implementation of the Quality Assurance Programme for the Privatized Hospital Support Services*

The objectives were as follows:

i.   To assist the MOH in monitoring the development of a quality assurance programme (QAP) for the hospital support services, as follows:

   a.   Assist MOH in establishing the required quality standards and appropriate key indicators for quality assurance for each of the five hospital support services.
   b.   Verify, validate, and evaluate the QAP reports submitted by the contractors.

    c.  Verify, validate, and report on the preventive and corrective action taken on the shortfalls in quality (SIQ) for the various quality assurance indicators.

    d.  Analyse and recommend to MOH any improvements to the QAP, and follow up action needed from the contractors.

ii.  To inspect and verify the QAP at the contract hospital level using appropriate field inspection checklists, and to issue NCRs for non-conformance in the implementation of the QAP

iii.  To attend meetings with the contract hospitals/contractors on related specific issues, as and when required

iv.  To prepare and submit the following:

    a.  The findings and observations made in the hospital monthly report to contract hospitals

    b.  Semi-annual summary reports on the status of the quality assurance programme for the privatized hospital support services.

## Assess Deductions and Verify Payments Due to the Contractors

The objectives were as follows:

i.  To advise the contract hospitals and to report on the use of the third-party services to carry out the non-conforming services of the contractor based on the concession agreement's non-conformance clauses, hereafter referred to as the contractor's third-party services.

    a.  To compile data pertaining to the implementation of the contractors' third-party services

    b.  To ensure that the payment due to the third-party service contractor/supplier was captured and deducted from the payments due to the contractor concerned, if the contractor concerned had not made the payments due to the third-party service contractor/supplier. Such deductions should be included in the consulting company's verification of works certifications (VWC) when verifying payments to the contractor concerned

    c.  To participate in meetings with the contract hospitals/contractors on related specific issues

ii.  To assess and report deductions for the contractor's non-conformance, as follows:

    a.  Assess the demerit points for deductions based on the complaints mapping report in accordance with the MOH guidelines for the application of the deduction formula.

    b.  Participate in the monthly contract-hospital-level Validation Committee meetings.

    c.  Participate in the state-level Validation Committee meetings as and when required to settle disputes raised by the contractor.

    d.  Assess and report on the deductions made for the contractors' instances of non-conformance that were validated by Validation Committee and based on the approved deduction mechanism.

iii.  To verify and report VWCs for payments due to the contractor, taking into consideration the deduction based on the approved deductions formula and the fees due to contractor's third-party services, and submit to the contract hospitals

iv.  To prepare and submit the following:

    a.  A monthly deduction assessment report (DAR) to contract hospitals

    b.  A monthly VWC to contract hospitals

    c.  A monthly summary report on deductions to MOH

    d.  Semi-annual summary reports on the implementation of the contractor's third-party services to MOH

    e.  January–June summary report on deductions and VWCs to MOH

    f.  Annual summary report on deductions and VWCs for the period January to December to MOH.

*Verify and Report Testing and Commissioning of New Equipment, Plant and Installation at Contract Hospitals*

The objectives were as follows:

i.  To verify the testing and commissioning (T&C) of new equipment, plants, and installations, consequent on the detailed T&C report by the contractor concerned, and as follows:

a. Inspect the T&C records and supporting documents submitted by the contractors. (Note: the contractors were required to witness and certify the T&C and thereafter register the new equipment, plant, and/or installation in the CMIS and the government standard inventory records.)

b. Verify the records of compliance with statutory regulations (including compliance with the Atomic Energy Licensing Act 304 for new irradiating apparatuses installed in contract hospitals).

c. Coordinate and/or attend meetings with the suppliers, contract hospitals and/or contractors on specific T&C requirements, as and when required.

ii. To prepare and submit the following:

a. A T&C report for each new piece of equipment, plant, or installation to the contract hospital concerned, as and when required

b. Semi-annual summary reports on verified T&C submitted to MOH

*Verify and Report on Condition Assessment of Installed Facilities at the Contract Hospitals*

The objectives were as follows:

i. To verify the condition of selected equipment, plant, installations, systems, and buildings at the contract hospital, consequent on the condition appraisal reports submitted by the contractors, and as follows:

a. To analyse and verify the data and other information submitted by the contractors in the condition appraisal reports submitted by the contractor as requested by the contract hospital concerned

b. Where there were no submissions from the contractors, the consulting company was to identify categories of equipment/systems and request the contractors to provide the condition appraisal reports

c. To submit recommendations to contract hospitals on equipment, plant, installations, systems, and buildings, which could be:

- Maintained by the contractor or upgraded, modified, and and/or refurbished as reimbursable works to the contractor or as minor works projects, in accordance with the classification of maintenance/reimbursable works, as defined and documented in the contract agreement
- Exempted from meeting the standards stipulated in the concession agreement (CA)
- Approved by MOH for beyond economic repair (BER) certification (for disposal of assets equal to or more than approved limits on the purchase value), demolished (for condemned buildings), or condemned and disposed of (for assets worth less than the approved limits on the purchase value)

   d. To coordinate and/or attend meetings with contract hospitals and contractors as and when required to resolve related issues

ii. To prepare and submit the following reports:

   a. A report on assessment and evaluation made with appropriate recommendations to the contract hospital concerned

   b. An inspection report on BER applications (BER2 report) to MOH for each request made by the contract hospital

   c. An annual summary report on inspections on BER applications submitted to MOH

   d. An annual summary report on inspections on exemption lists and condition appraisal submitted to MOH.

*Analyse and Report on the Assessment of the Contractor's Performance in the Provision of Hospital Support Services*

The objectives were as follows:

i. To compile, analyse, assess, and report on the contractor's performance in the provision of the hospital support services, as follows:

   a. To carry out a customer feedback survey (CFS) at all contract hospitals with an agreed frequency and schedule and based on a prescribed CFS questionnaire

b.   To assess the performance of the contractors once every six months (January to June and July to December), which should be based on the agreed mechanisms of assessment and carried out by the specialist consultants for the five hospital support services

c.   To coordinate and/or attend meetings with the MOH/contractors as and when required

ii.   To prepare and submit the following reports:

a.   A semi-annual CFS report at an agreed frequency to MOH

b.   A semi-annual contractor's performance assessment (CPA) report to MOH at an agreed frequency.

## 4.1.2. Consulting Services

*Provide Technical Advice as Needed Pertaining to the Privatized Hospital Support Services*

The objectives were as follows:

i.   To provide technical advice and/or recommendations on the following:

a.   Interpretation of the provision in the contractor's concession agreement and of the disputes raised and deviations introduced by the contractors, as and when requested or when the need arises

b.   Investigation into specific issues/problems encountered by the contract hospitals (such as linen loss, major breakdowns in facilities and biomedical equipment, power failure, etc.) based on the information and data provided by others (namely the contractor concerned, JKR, IKRAM, specialized testing agencies, a licensed surveyor, et al.), as well as verification of the data collected, analysing, preparing, and submitting technical reports with the findings and recommendations to the contract hospital/ state health department/MOH

c.   Assessment of the technical requirements and the costs of the privatized hospital support services based on the data and supporting documents presented by the contractors, and advice to the MOH on the contractors' requests for a review of rates for variations, as and when requested by MOH

d. Investigation into the requirements for the relocation/transfer of selected equipment from one contract hospital to another, and advising the MOH/state health department accordingly

e. The scope of service does not include specific investigations and in-depth studies that would require the services of expert and specialist technical personnel as well as provisions such as laboratory analysis, test equipment, performance-measuring instruments, etc. Such specific investigation and in-depth studies shall be carried out as reimbursable services.

ii. To evaluate and advise MOH on the utilization of specific materials, chemicals, and equipment in the provision of the hospital support services, as requested by MOH and as follows:

a. To prepare and submit reports to MOH on the evaluation of and recommendations for the materials, chemicals, and equipment proposed by the contractors, as requested by MOH, based on the data and information submitted by the contractors

b. To compile annually the list of approved materials, chemicals, and equipment for use in the provision of the hospital support services, as well as to evaluate and recommend to MOH the changes required as deemed necessary

iii. To review the approved project operations guidelines and procedures needed for the monitoring, certifying, and evaluating of the hospital support services and to evaluate the implementation of the agreed deduction formula pertaining to the provision of the hospital support services, as follows:

a. To carry out an annual review and evaluation of approved project operations guidelines (POGs) and project operations procedures (POPs) as set out in the CA, based on the assessment of the implementation of the hospital support services, contractors' disputes, and other forms of assessment

b. To submit recommendations to MOH on proposed improvements, amendments, modifications, and deletions (as appropriate) to the POGs and POPs

c. To assist MOH in the development of new POGs or POPs pertaining to hospital support services, as per request

iv. To assess, evaluate, and report on the performance, effectiveness, and efficiency of selected category equipment (FEMS and BEMS), up to a ceiling of three pieces of FEMS equipment or three FEMS systems at contract hospitals, as follows:

a. To assess, evaluate, and advise MOH on a selected category of equipment and systems (FEMS and BEMS) based on agreement by MOH

b. Base the assessment on various data, including specifications, purchase and maintenance costs, safety and performance data obtained from the contractors, and feedback from hospital personnel. Wherever possible and practicable, comparison should be made with data available from similar facilities elsewhere in the country or overseas

v. To coordinate and/or attend meetings with MOH/contractors on related specific issues, as and when required

vi. To prepare and submit the following reports:

a. Technical report or written technical advice on the investigation of specific issues/problems to contract hospital concerned/MOH within the agreed time frame

b. Technical report on the assessment of the technical requirements and the costs of the privatized hospital support services, contractors' fee review, and contractors' rates for variations

c. Technical report to the contract hospitals/state health department concerned on the relocation or transfer of equipment, as and when requested

d. Technical evaluation report on the utilization of materials, chemicals, and equipment in the hospital support services (BEMS excluded), complete with an evaluation of the annual list of approved materials, chemicals, and equipment

e. Revisions to existing POGs/POPs and drafts of a new POG/POP as and when requested by MOH

f. Annual report on the recommended changes to the POGs and POPs or the development of a new POG or POP

g. Assessment report for select categories of FEMS and BEMS equipment/system to MOH

h. Quarterly summary report to MOH on technical advice.

*Verify Notified Variations and Recommend Fees for Verified Variations*

The objectives were as follows:

i. To inspect and verify all notified variations as well as to assess and recommend to MOH the fees payable to the contractors for the verified variations, as follows:

a. To inspect and verify the variations in accordance with the guidelines on the management of variations in contract hospitals based on records submitted by the contractors

b. To verify the rates for variations in the quantity of hospital support services as proposed by the contractors, and to recommend appropriate rates for the consideration of MOH, based on supporting data provided by the contractors as well as costing norms obtained from other agencies

c. To estimate and recommend the variations in the fees for the additions, deletions, and/or upgraded facilities, based on a compiled and verified Variations Verification form (VVF) and supporting data submitted by the contractors, and the approved rates

d. To coordinate and/or attend meetings with MOH and/or contractors as required

ii. To prepare and submit semi-annual reports on variations in the fees for the contractors' services to MOH.

*Provide Briefing and Training to MOH/Contract Hospital Personnel*

The objectives were as follows:

i.  To provide training to selected MOH personnel on the latest technology pertaining to the hospital support services as well as briefing on the roles of contractors, consulting company, and contract hospitals to key personnel of the contract hospitals, as follows:

    a.  To organize annual regional workshop sessions in order to brief the key personnel from the MOH/state health department/contract hospitals on various aspects of the hospital support services, as well as on the changes to the approved MOH guidelines and project operations guidelines/procedures
    b.  To provide briefings to newly appointed directors/liaison officers of contract hospitals within sixty days of their appointment
    c.  To provide technology-transfer training to selected MOH personnel pertaining to the five hospital support services and based on the annual training programme approved by MOH
    d.  To coordinate and/or attend meetings as and when required

ii. To prepare and submit the following:

    a.  An annual training programme to MOH
    b.  A semi-annual summary report on the training and briefing activities carried out to MOH

*Assist in the Implementation of Approved Minor Works as and When Requested by MOH/Contract Hospitals*

The objectives were as follows:

i.  To assist MOH/contract hospitals in the preparation of design and quotation documents and in the monitoring of the implementation of approved minor works projects within quotation limits as set out by the Ministry of Finance, as requested by the MOH/contract hospitals. Projects requiring specialized investigations such as topographic survey, site survey, soil investigations, structural testing, electrical load measurements, as-built drawings of existing buildings/structures, etc., as well as input from others (specialized service providers et al.), shall be considered as reimbursable services. The activities under this subscope were as follows:

a.  To prepare and submit quotation documents complete with specifications and drawings
b.  To prepare and submit quotation evaluation reports
c.  To monitor projects under construction (where standing supervision was required for a specific project, this would fall under reimbursable services)
d.  To verify progress payment/final payment through the issuance of a VWC
e.  To verify work completion through the issuance of the certificate of practical completion (CPC)
f.  To report progress on the implementation of approved projects to contract hospitals in the hospital monthly reports
g.  To prepare and submit to MOH/contract hospital a quarterly summary report on the status of approved minor works projects

ii.  To compile and submit annual lists of proposed minor works at the contract hospitals for the following year, as follows:

a.  To identify projects for the improvement of facilities, equipment, and systems, based on the requests made by the contract hospitals/ MOH or from the condition appraisal reports submitted by the contractors. The consultant will carry out preliminary plans and cost estimates and provide them to the contract hospitals for consideration
b.  To prepare and submit an annual list of proposed minor works ranked in order of urgency and priority with estimated costs to the contract hospitals for consideration and implementation
c.  To prepare and submit a yearly master list of all proposed minor works for the following year, ranked in order of priority with estimated costs to MOH for consideration and implementation

iii. To verify the quotations submitted for reimbursable works by the contractors or minor works by any third-party contractors appointed by the contract hospital, as requested by the contract hospital concerned/ MOH, as follows:

    a.  To evaluate and advise contract hospitals on the scope of works and the prices in the quotations, as requested by the contract hospital concerned

    b.  To monitor the progress of project implementation

    c.  To verify work remaining until completion

    d.  To prepare and submit a semi-annual summary report on the status of the projects by others to the contract hospitals/MOH

## 4.2. Organization of the Consulting Company

To effectively manage the monitoring and supervision of the concession companies at the different zones, SIHAT's organization is divided on the basis of zone coverage and task assignments. At the top of the organizational chart is the chief operating officer (COO), followed by two project technical managers (PTM), each responsible for monitoring and consulting respectively. All the zone managers report to the PTM for monitoring, whereas the PTM for consulting has a different function, namely to manage specialist consultants and consultants for special assignments such as objective assessment studies, equipment assessments, contractor's performance assessments, etc. The typical organizational chart of SIHAT is shown in Figure 8, below.

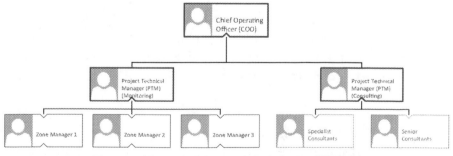

Figure 8 **Typical organizational chart of SIHAT**

## Roles and Responsibilities

Roles and responsibilities of the various posts in the organizational chart is as given below.

### Chief Operating Officer

The chief operating officer was responsible to SIHAT's board of directors and to its Management and Audit Committee for the overall planning, implementation, and monitoring of the operating activities in accordance with the requirements of the SIHAT–MOH agreement, with the following responsibilities:

i. Report on the progress of all operating activities
ii. Plan the utilization of manpower provided to deliver the services according to the requirements and performance indicators in the SIHAT–MOH agreement
iii. Manage the project's operations team at SIHAT headquarters and other zones
iv. Ensure that the project's operations team implement the management information system (MIS) and quality management system (QMS) according to established requirements and future improvement
v. Monitor the performance of the project's operations team at the headquarters and other zones
vi. Liaise with the MOH officials at all levels, especially at MOH HQ, state level, and major hospitals
vii. Carry out any other duties as directed by the board of directors

### Project Technical Manager (Monitor)

The project technical manager (PTM) (monitor) was responsible to the COO for the overall planning, coordination, and evaluation of the monitoring services provided to the contract hospitals and MOH. The PTM's job scope was as follows:

i. Coordinate, delegate, and distribute assignments to the zone managers
ii. Ensure that zones carry out the scheduled visits to all contract hospitals as well as the various monitoring functions, complying with approved procedures, guidelines, and other policy decisions made by MOH

iii. Ensure that zones complete and submit all reports correctly and timely

iv. Ensure that the zones collect and submit on time other data and information required by the hospitals, HQ, and MOH

v. Assist the zones in carrying out technical audits on the five privatized hospital support services at contract hospitals

vi. Assist the zones in conducting investigations into specific facility-related problems as and when requested by the zones

vii. Provide technical advice to MOH, the state, and/or hospitals as and when required

viii. Attend meetings at MOH, state, and hospital level as and when required

ix. Compile the relevant reports and supporting data for submission to MOH/state health department/hospitals

x. Carry out any other related assignments as instructed by the COO

*Project Technical Manager (Consulting)*

The PTM (consultant) was responsible to the COO for the overall planning, coordination, and evaluation of consultancy services provided to MOH and the contract hospitals, with responsibilities as follows:

i. Coordinate the activities of the HQ technical team, which includes but is not limited to contractors' performance assessment, objective assessment at selected hospitals, training for MOH/SIHAT personnel, and providing technical advice on five support services.

ii. Provide technical advice to MOH, the state health department, and/or hospitals on the following:

    a. Resolution of contractors' disputes and interpretation of various provisions of the contractors' concession agreement (particularly TRPI, MAP, and the deduction formula)

    b. Review of contractors' requests for fee review, cost estimates of the services, variations, and omissions

    c. Recommendations to improve the services

    d. Resolution of contractors' disputes encountered at the hospital level, and interpretation of TRPI, MAP, and the deduction formula

iii. Coordinate investigations into specific problems, contractors' disputes, and incidences, as well as interpret the contractors' concession agreement, pertaining to five hospital services based on requests from MOH, hospitals, and SIHAT personnel at zone and HQ level

iv. Coordinate the review and revision of various guidelines, procedures, and work instructions as well as prepare other guidelines/procedures required for the smooth implementation of the monitoring functions at the zone level

v. Coordinate and facilitate the compilation and preparation of estimates required for contractors' fee reviews and fees for variations

vi. Coordinate the implementation of all approved reimbursable services

vii. Coordinate the preparation of project proposals, plans, design documents, and quotation documents for the minor works projects, as per request from contract hospitals or MOH

viii. Compile, review, and submit an annual programme for proposed minor works projects to MOH based on data obtained from the zones

ix. Attend meetings at MOH, state, and hospital level as and when required

x. Compile relevant reports and supporting data for submission to MOH/state health department/hospitals

xi. Carry out any other related assignments as instructed by the COO

*Zone Managers*

Zone managers, senior consultants in the company, were responsible to the project technical manager for monitoring all aspects of zone operations. Their job functions were as follows:

i. Manage the overall operations, administration, operating expenses, and performance of the zone

ii. Plan, coordinate, assign, implement, and evaluate the activities of the technical personnel, based on the agreed key result area (KRA) and key performance indicators (KPI), ensuring efficient and effective implementation of the SIHAT concession agreement (SCA) activities at each contract hospital in the zone, and also complying with approved guidelines and procedures

iii. Ensure that technical personnel carry out the scheduled visits to contract hospitals based on the agreed frequency

iv.   Participate in meetings or discussions held by MOH/state health department/contract hospitals, as well as prepare notes of the discussion/minutes of meetings, submitting these to the relevant authorities, with copies extended to the PTM (monitor)

v.   Organize regular meetings with zone technical personnel

vi.   Coordinate or conduct investigations into specific problems, disputes, and instances of contractor non-performance and non-compliance or as requested by contract hospitals/SIHAT HQ through scheduled or unscheduled visits to contract hospitals/contractors' facilities on a random basis

vii.   Liaise, coordinate with, and maintain a cordial working environment with the contract hospitals, contractors, JKR, et al., at the zone level

viii.   Disseminate and implement approved policies, decisions, and directives made by MOH/SIHAT HQ, and provide feedback if necessary

ix.   Provide technical advice to contract hospitals/zone personnel on the SCA, contractors' concession/supplementary agreements, and other matters pertaining to the zone manager's professional expertise

x.   Coordinate, compile, prepare, and submit relevant reports as required in SCA's/SIHAT's quality management system and as requested by MOH/SIHAT HQ

xi.   Verify technical reports prepared by technical personnel at the zone level, ensuring the accuracy, completeness, and correctness of supporting data/information

xii.   Carry out other tasks assigned by the PTM (monitor) from time to time

*Specialist Consultants*

The specialist consultants were responsible to the PTM (consultant) for activities in the field of their expertise in relation to the hospital support services under FEMS, BEMS, and CWMS. Their responsibilities were as follows:

i.   Carry out a contractor performance assessment (CPA) by evaluating data on third-party services engaged by the hospitals, deductions made, selected data of service output as extracted from the CMIS, and the results of the customer feedback survey

    ii.  Carry out an objective assessment of the services at selected hospitals, which includes a review of the contractor's manpower, documentation, training level, and awareness levels

    iii.  Provide technical advice to MOH, the state health departments, and/or hospitals on the following matters:

        a.  Resolution of contractors' disputes encountered at the hospital level, and interpretation of various provisions of the contractors' concession agreement, particularly the TRPI, MAP, and deduction formula

        b.  Review of contractors' requests for fee review, cost estimates of the services, variations, and omissions

        c.  Recommendations to improve services

        d.  Review of selected HSIP with a view towards recommending improvements to the services

    iv.  Attend meetings of the technical committee, the technical subcommittee, and others at MOH/contract hospitals, and submit notes of the discussions at meetings for onward submission to relevant authorities

    v.  Provide technical training to SIHAT's technical personnel as well as prepare guidelines, procedures, and checklists where deemed necessary

    vi.  Prepare relevant technical reports for submission to MOH/state health department/contract hospitals

    vii.  Carry out any related assignments as instructed by the COO

*Senior Consultants*

The senior consultants were responsible to the respective PTMs at the consulting or monitoring department. Their duties included the following:

    i.  Assist the PTM concerned in carrying out relevant activities at HQ/zone level, including unscheduled visits to selected contract hospitals to conduct investigations into specific problems, contractors' disputes, and contractor non-performance and non-compliance, and where required, issue NCRs where and when required

    ii.  Inspect and verify the services and the contractor's performance during the scheduled and unscheduled visits to the assigned contract hospital(s) to ensure compliance with the TRPI, the MAP, and statutory requirements, using the appropriate field inspection checklists (FIC) and issuing NCRs as necessary

iii. Participate in meetings with the contractors and/or MOH at the HQ, zone, state, or contract hospital level to discuss and resolve specific technical problems

iv. Carry out other activities, such as verification of testing and commissioning of new equipment or facilities, inspecting for beyond economic repair (BER) certification, attending to minor works projects, etc., as directed by the relevant PTM

v. Prepare layout plans, detailed designs, specifications, tender drawings, and tender documents, for approved projects for MOH, the state health department, and contract hospitals for those consultants involved in minor works projects

vi. Compile, analyse, and evaluate proposed minor works projects.

## 4.3. Zone Coverage

In order to effectively supervise and monitor the performance of the three concession companies undertaking the privatized hospital support services, SIHAT divided its monitoring activities into geographical zones based on state coverage. Thus, in all there were seven zones created, as follows:

a) Zone 1 for Kuala Lumpur and Selangor
b) Zone 2A for Penang, Kedah, and Perlis
c) Zone 2B for Perak
d) Zone 3 for Negeri Sembilan, Johor, and Melaka
e) Zone 4 for Pahang, Terengganu, and Kelantan
f) Zone 5 for Sarawak
g) Zone 6 for Sabah and Labuan Island

## 4.4. Reimbursable Services

Reimbursable services were services provided to MOH upon their request or as requested by the consultant with the prior approval of SIHAT. The chargeable fee was based on a schedule within the consulting agreement, which was on a man-months basis with multipliers to cover for administration, employees provident fund (EPF), social security organization (SOCSO), etc. The items covered in the reimbursable services were as follows:

a) Prepare preliminary/detailed planning, detailed design, drawings, specifications, tender documents, and tender evaluation reports for projects in existing contract hospitals that exceed the quotation limits of MOH, such as the following:

   i.   New buildings and/or facilities
   ii.  Supply and installation of systems, plant, equipment, or other installations (new, upgraded, or replacement)
   iii. Refurbishment, extension, or renovation of existing buildings

b) Supervise projects that exceed the quotation limits set out by MOH in existing contract hospitals, including testing and commissioning as well as certification of works completion, as follows:

   i.   New buildings and/or facilities
   ii.  Supply and installation of systems, plant, equipment, or other installations (new, upgraded, or replacement)
   iii. Refurbishment, extension, or renovation of existing buildings

c) Witness and report on the testing and commissioning of equipment and installations in replacement contract hospitals and new hospitals, health institutions, and/or facilities

d) Prepare the pre-qualification documents, scope of works, specifications, tender documents, technical data, bills of quantities, and tender evaluation reports for the contracting of the hospital support services in a new hospital, health institution, and/or facility

e) Carry out the activities as requested by MOH during the takeover of new buildings in existing contract hospitals, replacement hospitals, and new hospitals, institutions, and/or facilities

f) Assess, verify, document, and report on the transfer of takeover assets from the contract hospital to the contractor, and submit reports thereto

g) Provide expatriate consultant services to MOH on hospital support services

h) Provide specialized investigation services such as topographic survey, site survey, soil investigation, structure testing, electrical load measurements, and submission of plans with endorsement from relevant qualified persons (professional engineer, professional architect, et al.) for approval to the relevant statutory agencies wherever required, and prepare as-built drawings for existing buildings/structures

## 4.5. Training

According to the contract with MOH, SIHAT was to conduct a series of training sessions over the contract period for MOH personnel at hospitals and on MOH premises. The intent of the training sessions was for hospitals and MOH personnel to have a better understanding of the contractors' concession agreement; to organize technology transfer training pertaining to the five privatized hospital support services for MOH personnel and the consultant; and to allow for the continuous education and upgrading of knowledge and expertise pertaining to hospital support services of the consulting personnel. Pursuant to this, the training programme was divided into workshop sessions for MOH personnel, technology transfer training pertaining to the five privatized hospital support services, and continued technical education for the consulting company's technical personnel.

The workshop sessions were useful for briefing the newly appointed directors/ liaison officers of contract hospitals. The objective of the workshop sessions was to ensure that the key personnel from contract hospitals/the state health department/MOH had a clear understanding of the scope of the privatized hospital support services, which include the following subjects:

a) Requirements of the hospital support services as per the contractor's concession agreement, supplementary agreement, TRPI, and MAP
b) The deduction formula
c) Requirement of the hospital-specific implementation plan
d) The use of the CMIS to monitor the hospital support services
e) Other specific issues and disputes raised by the contractors pertaining to the privatized hospital support services

Technology transfer training was conducted through attendance of international conferences overseas, regional or national conferences, seminars and/or workshops, and short courses organized locally on subjects pertaining to the five privatized hospital support services. The courses could be organized by local institutions, universities, professional bodies, and/or the consulting company.

Continued education for the consulting company included in-house courses provided by specialist consultants or by external organizations such as professional bodies, universities, and institutions.

# Chapter 5

# Management Information System

## 5.1. Background

This chapter will not discuss the mechanics of the management information system (MIS) used by the contractors, the MOH, SIHAT, and the hospitals. Rather, the chapter will look into features of the information system that were established in the management of the hospital support services by the parties related to it.

As part of the obligations of the concession agreement, the concession companies that were awarded the contract were responsible for the establishment of a management information system for all the hospitals and health institutions. The system that was established was called the centralized management information system, which is an integrated nationwide system. The contractors initially established their own basic management information system (MIS) to manage the entire project and to track the works performed for all five services individually. The basic management information systems of the three contractors were then linked to the centralized management information system (CMIS) for further consolidation and integration.

The original CMIS, known as CMIS Version 1.0, had several shortcomings, which limited its use in the management of the project. Since then, a revised and improved version was created: CMIS Version 2, 2002. The contractors then renamed the CMIS Version 2, 2002, referring to it as *e-urushospital*. The CMIS Version 2 was developed as an executive information system (EIS), with the main objective of providing online reports and records about the assets of the contract hospitals as well as about the performance of the five privatized hospital support services.

The system was developed using the latest Web-based technology available and using the Internet as the communication medium. The Internet technology was chosen to ensure that users would be able to access the CMIS from anywhere in the country and internationally. Access to the system was controlled by four levels of user ID and password, namely the national, consortium, state, and hospital levels.

Information gathered into the CMIS was communicated from the basic MIS of the three contractors and stored in a central server, which was located at the Ministry of Health.

The CMIS was designed and developed using the state-of-the-art electronic data warehouse, which provided parallel access and fast delivery. The CMIS was a user-friendly, integrated, comprehensive, timely, single-source management information system. The CMIS data warehouse operated predominantly on Microsoft Windows 2000 server and Microsoft SQL Server 2000 for a relational database management system.

The system was connected to over 2,000 computer terminals covering 150 locations (the Ministry of Health, contractors' off-site facilities, and SIHAT HQ/zone/site offices), through which data were refreshed daily and made available to all parties accessing the system.

Information received from the servers of the three contractors was processed, sorted, and compiled, and thereafter transformed into meaningful and measurable information prior to being transmitted to the CMIS.

The CMIS empowered all parties to monitor and measure the contractors' performance. By automating the data transfer and compilation, CMIS facilitated better documentation and planning, and improved the measuring and tracking of compliances, service outputs, and outcomes.

## 5.2. Access

Visitors had accessibility to the CMIS's Open Web home page. There were two sets of menus available for further viewing of the home page, namely the top menu and the left-side menu. The top menu consisted of the selection of the five hospital support services (HSS). Clicking any one of the top menu selections led to an information page about the selected service(s).

The side menu on the left side of the home page included the selection to write up other information. Clicking any one of the side-menu selections led to the following:

a) **About HSS**: A brief synopsis about the hospital support services
b) **SIHAT**: Links to SIHAT's website, which provided further information on the services provided by SIHAT
c) **Feedback**: Enabled the visitor to send any feedback concerning the CMIS to the system administrator
d) **Webmail**: For MOH use only
e) **The hit number**: Number of times the CMIS had been accessed

To access the CMIS, the user had to key his or her user ID and password in the slot for login at the right side of the screen. All authorized users of the CMIS were provided with a user ID and password, which were based on the security level assigned by MOH. The security level for CMIS was divided into four categories, as follows:

i. **Access to CMIS at contract hospital level**: Users in this category could access information for only their particular hospital. Users in this category included the hospital directors, the contractor's branch managers, and the SIHAT consultant.
ii. **Access to CMIS at state level**: Users in this category could access information for all contract hospitals within their particular state. Users in this category included state health directors, the contractor's regional/area manager, and SIHAT's zone manager.
iii. **Access to CMIS at consortium (contractor) level**: Users in this category could access information for all contract hospitals within the particular concession company. Users in this category were the key personnel at the contractor's headquarters.
iv. **Access to CMIS at national level**: Users in this category could access information for all contract hospitals nationwide. Users in this category included the director of engineering services, members of the MOH Supervision (*Kawalselia*) Unit, key personnel from the Division of Engineering Services, selected key personnel from other divisions of MOH involved in the privatized HSS, and key personnel at SIHAT headquarters.

Once the user was successfully logged in, the CMIS home page would be displayed. The security level of the user ID and password determined the information that could be assessed.

The top menu of the CMIS home page provided the following selections:

a) **FEMS**: Provided detailed information with respect to facility engineering maintenance services that could be inspected
b) **BEMS**: Provided detailed information with respect to biomedical engineering maintenance services
c) **CLS**: Provided detailed information with respect to cleansing services
d) **CWMS**: Provided detailed information with respect to clinical waste management services
e) **LLS**: Provided detailed information with respect to linen and laundry services
f) **Financial and deductions**: Provided detailed information on deductions, invoices, and payments received
g) **Hospital info**: Provided basic information about the hospital, including pictures
h) **QAP**: Reported on the contractors' quality assurance programme. Provided information on the QAP's (quality assurance programme) indicators, data on shortfall in quality (SIQ), and the corrective action that should be taken to improve quality
i) **Logout**: Enabled users to log out of the CMIS

The bottom menu of the CMIS home page provided the following selections:

a) **Change password**: Enabled the user to change his or her password
b) **Feedback**: Provided an email compose screen which allowed the visitor to the home page to send any feedback via email directly to the CMIS administrator in order to provide any feedback regarding the CMIS
c) **Site map**: Displayed a list of records and analyses available in the CMIS for each service. The site map was also the shortcut; it linked to these reports without the user's having to go through the home page of each of the services
d) **Schedule IV**: Displayed a lists of reports and analyses available in the CMIS for each service based on Schedule IV reports. The Schedule

IV was also the shortcut to these reports, without the user's having to go through the home page of each service

e) **Links**: Listed links to the websites of SIHAT, the Emergency Care Research Institute (ECRI), the three contractors, and the Web developer

## 5.3. Reports

Reports in the CMIS were generated in two format types: report and analysis. Report formats were text formats which provided the required information in preformatted form. Generally, these text reports contained multilevel reports from the summary level to the more detailed level, with various levels of drill down.

Analysis reports were displayed in pivot table format. They were accompanied by graphs in some cases. The user was allowed to customize and generate specific reports. Analysis was dynamic; users could manoeuvre the information and generate the reports and graphs according to their needs.

Users of the CMIS were allowed restricted viewing of the reports according to the security password allocated to them. For example, the user who logged in with the password for Hospital A was allowed to view the information for Hospital A only.

Listed below, in Tables 10, 11, 12 and 13, are reports generated in the CMIS for the monitoring of the five hospital support services. The source of this information is *User Manual for CMIS Version 2, 2002*. The reports below are not exhaustive; additional or amended reports could be added as the need arose.

Table 10 **Reports for facility and biomedical engineering maintenance services**

| Item | Report name | Contents | Remarks |
|------|-------------|----------|---------|
| 1. | Asset register details | Mandatory fields in asset register: asset number, manufacturer, model, serial number, asset name, purchase cost, date of supply, department, location, status, condition, warranty expiry date, capacity<br><br>All equipment requiring DOSH certification with registration number to be recorded<br><br>Cumulative maintenance cost and equipment history were updated progressively | Purchase cost, or date to be estimated if cost is not available<br><br>Fields not required for a given asset were flagged "not applicable" |
| 2. | Asset summary listing | Summary information extracted from item 1, above | Drilling down provided asset details |
| 3. | Works requests | Listed requests responded to on time and responded to late for the selected month | Drilling down provided request details |
| 4. | Work orders | Scheduled work order for PPM, routine inspection, and scheduled corrective maintenance<br><br>Unscheduled work order for breakdown, corrective maintenance, safety and performance, user request | Routine inspection was available for FEMS only<br><br>Safety and performance test report for BEMS only |
| 5. | Work orders summary | Scheduled work order for PPM, routine inspection, and scheduled corrective maintenance<br><br>Unscheduled work order for breakdown, corrective maintenance, safety and performance, user request | Routine inspection was available for FEMS only<br><br>Safety and performance test report for BEMS only |

| 6. | Summary of work orders in progress | Scheduled work order for PPM, routine inspection, scheduled corrective maintenance<br><br>Unscheduled work order for breakdown, corrective maintenance, safety and performance, user request | In-progress work orders could be viewed by selecting the option "outstanding more than fifteen days"<br><br>Routine inspection was available for FEMS only<br><br>Safety and performance test report for BEMS only or "within 15 days" option |
| 7. | Summary of work orders completed | Scheduled work order for PPM, routine inspection, and scheduled corrective maintenance<br><br>Unscheduled work order for breakdown, corrective maintenance, safety and performance, user request | One could choose "completed more than 15 days" or "completed within 15 days" for unscheduled work orders<br><br>As for scheduled work orders, the information was under "completed within schedule" or was grouped in "completed not to schedule" |
| 8. | Summary of outstanding work orders | Scheduled work order for PPM, routine inspection, and scheduled corrective maintenance<br><br>Unscheduled work order for breakdown, corrective maintenance, safety and performance, user request | Unscheduled work orders were those as listed in item 7, above<br><br>Scheduled work orders were those listed under "remaining for the month" |
| 9. | Stock register | Listed stock code, description, and balance at each store | Hospital users were able to view the details of their respective store. Central store and warehouse information was shown to a user with consortium- or national-level access |
| 10. | Planned preventive maintenance schedule | Information shown was to be based on code, scheduled date, and checklist reference number | This information was only shown for schedules that were already generated. PPM details could be viewed from the Work Orders screen once the PPM came due |

| 11. | Contract out register | Listed contract number, contractor, period of contract, and types of equipment contracted for the selected period | |
|-----|----|----|----|

## Table 11  **Reports for cleansing services**

| Item | Report name | Contents | Remarks |
|------|-------------|----------|---------|
| 1. | Daily performance report | The report showed all non-conformances for the following:<br>• Cleansing as well as collection not done and done not according to schedule<br>• Insufficient consumables | Data extracted from daily cleansing activity records |
| 2. | Weekly routine quality checklist | The reports showed the number of user locations, parameters, satisfactory, not satisfactory by hospital, user area, user location, and document number | |
| 3. | Monthly summarized report | The report showed all non-conformances for the following:<br>• Cleansing as well as collection not done and done not to schedule<br>• Insufficient consumables | Data extracted from daily cleansing activity records |
| 4. | Cleansing request report | Summary report showed the number of requests done, and outstanding, by hospital and user location | Select option "normal" for requests in CMIS |
| 5. | Emergency maintenance report | Summary report showed the number of requests done, and outstanding, by hospital and user location | Select option "emergency" for requests in CMIS |

Table 12 **Reports for linen and laundry services**

| Item | Report name | Contents | Remarks |
|---|---|---|---|
| 1. | Monthly hospital linen usage report | Summary report showed quantity of linen requested, quantity issued, quantity rejected, quantity replaced, and shortfalls, by month and hospital | Drilling down provided further details of linen based on linen item, user location, date, or clean linen number |
| 2. | Condemnation report | The report provided information about condemnation of linen items and the reasons for condemnation | Linen condemnation was only performed at the laundry or the regional linen store. As such, these data could not be retrieved at hospital level.<br><br>Only users with national or consortium access could view this report |
| 3. | Linen stock listing | The report gave data on linen requirements according to the HSIP.<br><br>It provided the description, material, size, and piping of each linen item | |
| 4. | Analysis report on losses | These reports gave data on weights of clean linen issued, soiled linen weight, factored weight of soiled linen collected, and value of linen loss<br><br>Drilling down provided information on linen loss by hospital, by month, and by user location | Subjected to final linen loss formula adopted |
| 5. | Linen inventory report | This report provided data on quantity linen inspected, quantity condemned, current HSIP stock level, current quantity at hand, and current value at hand | Report could be viewed by users with consortium-level access |

| 6. | Tensile strength report | This report gave detailed information on the type of linen tested and the acceptance status from MOH | Linen compliance test performed for samples taken from regional stores |
|---|---|---|---|
| 7. | pH level test | This report provided data on non-compliance of each laundry machine at each laundry | pH level test performed at laundry only. Data entry was only done for instances of non-conformance |
| 8. | Pathological test | This test was represented by thermal disinfectant temperature meeting specific requirements. This was recorded under the "thermal disinfection test" column | |

## Table 13 **Reports for clinical waste management services**

| Item | Report name | Contents | Remarks |
|---|---|---|---|
| 1. | Validity of certificate report | Provided listing of licenses and certificates by incinerator and the number of expired ones<br><br>The report showed:<br>- License/certificate number<br>- Description<br>- Expiry date<br>- Class/grade | Licenses for the incinerators were only available for users with consortium- or national-level access |
| 2. | Validated complaint report | Listed summary and detail of complaints by hospital<br><br>Validated complaints with the status of "valid and closed" or "not valid and closed" | Complaint details could be accessed by drilling down from the summary screen.<br><br>Three sources of complaints:<br>- MOH<br>- CMIS by automatic complaint generation<br>- NCR |

| 3. | Weighing report | Provided number of bins and weight by hospital | Drilling down listed number of bins, net weight, and consignment note by date. Clicking *Consignment Note* provided details of the consignment note |
|---|---|---|---|
| 4. | Record sheet report | This report provided a summary of bins collected and the collection status | |
| 5. | Waste generation monthly summary report | Report showed total weight and number of bins collected by hospital based on daily waste record sheet (DWRS) | Further drill down was available by date or consignment note |
| 6. | Tracing of consignment report | This report showed information on number of bins and total weight transported, number of bins and total weight received at the incinerator and total weight strayed beyond tolerance | MOH to set tolerance level |
| 7. | Transportation report | Report listed vehicle number and the number of incidents by hospital. Clicking on Vehicle Number provided details on date, description, report number, date submitted and remarks | Date submitted referred to the date of the incident |
| 8. | Regional incinerator compliance testing report | Report showed the listing of compliance, date document number, status of compliance, date submitted to MOH, and date submitted to DOE | Drilling down provided details on parameters, unit of measurement, permissible level, and the results achieved |
| 9. | Transportation reconciliation report | Report listed the number of delays for each hospital | Drilling down provided details on date, driver, vehicle number, consignment note number, and remarks |

| 10. | Payment received audit report | Report on CWMS fees billed and payment status by hospital | Drilling down provided information on invoice number, invoice date, service fee, service tax, invoice amount, date paid, and amount paid |
| --- | --- | --- | --- |
| 11. | Internal waste delivery record | Report listed weight of waste received from other MOH facilities | Other MOH facilities meant clinics outside the hospital premises |

# Chapter 6

# Comments and Conclusion

## 6.1. General

Healthcare facilities, unlike other commercial or office facilities, are very complicated because of their requirement to match the different services offered. The facilities, in addition to functioning like normal buildings, need to be designed in such a way to meet clinical requirements, to process flows such as the movement of clinical waste, to adapt to patient flow, and to provide critical services. The engineering support services system, like the system for medical gases, a critical and uninterrupted power supply, the air-conditioning system, and other mechanical systems, has to be designed to meet medical and clinical requirements.

The biggest challenge faced by healthcare facilities is the constant change in requirements, especially those arising from technological advances and improved standard requirements, for effective hospital operation and maintenance. Hospitals normally expand at the same site to serve the local population. An increase in population will increase the demand for more beds and services. As such, hospitals need to have a long-term view to meet the expansion requirements. Facilities managers have to be aware of these requirements if they are to succeed in managing the hospital facilities and making provisions in their design planning.

When the government of Malaysia proposed the privatization of the five support services in government hospitals, the tasks and responsibilities handed to the Ministry of Health (MOH) and the concession companies were enormous and daunting.

At the onset of the privatization, engineering maintenance for both facilities and biomedical engineering was very much ad hoc, daily, and reactive. This led to many problems, such as the breakdown of equipment that had not been attended to. Spare parts for critical services were not available in a timely manner. As such, hospital services suffered – and attention to patient care suffered as well. These were some issues faced by the proponents for a new system of hospital support services. The proposal for the new system at the time was to move from a practice of reactive maintenance to a practice of preventive maintenance for both the facility and biomedical equipment, at least to address and minimize potential breakdowns or equipment failures.

Thus, when the new contract agreement was drafted, the proponents for the new hospital support services included in the contract's core various elements and clauses in support of preventive maintenance, as found in the conditions of the contract, the technical requirements and performance indicators (TRPI), the master agreed procedures (MAP), hospital-specific implementation plans (HSIPs), project operations guidelines (POGs), etc. This course of action was considered prudent to upgrade the facility and biomedical services, as time was needed to train personnel associated with the hospital so that they would come to understand the merits of good engineering practices and services. Preventive maintenance is one step better than reactive daily maintenance, so the experience and knowledge gained over the years of implementing preventive maintenance should enable the maintenance personnel to move up the scale to proactive maintenance at a later stage. A combination of an effective system and measures for preventive and proactive maintenance was hoped to lead to better hospital services for patient care. This has actually materialized; hospital support services have improved tremendously since the implementation of the contract agreement.

## 6.2. Issues

For a large-scale project of this magnitude, it is not surprising that issues and problems arose in the course of implementation and execution for all parties concerned. This chapter will omit the minor issues but will discuss some of the major issues and problems.

### 6.2.1. Manpower Needs

Finding suitable, qualified and experienced personnel to administer, supervise, and manage the contract was a challenge for the concession companies (CCs).

The reason for the difficulty in manpower resourcing was that this type of contract was new to the Ministry of Health, especially at the beginning of the concession period. Although the existing hospitals had engineers, technical staff, and technical personnel, the experience of implementing the project was new to many within the hospital – and to the contractors as well. Established government hospitals in larger cities may have had trained and experienced technical personnel, but at district and rural hospitals personnel of this type were lacking. Upon the award of the project to the concession companies, a programme of absorption of existing technical staff from the government hospitals to the CCs was undertaken as stipulated in the contract agreement. In addition, the CCs went on a recruitment drive, seeking personnel from the market to address the manpower needs of the hospital support services (HSS). This effort partially alleviated the shortage of manpower in the HSS during the initial phase of the project.

Personnel recruited for the project had to understand not only the technical issues of engineering but also the intricacy and complexity of administering the contract. Mistakes and disputes in the interim period were many, incurring losses to both the CCs and the government. Disputes arose in many of the monthly payment validation meetings to establish monthly progressive payments to the CCs. Some of these disputes were acrimonious, with no solution found.

The disputes arose because in this project, the mode of payment was by deduction formula, whereby the contractor was penalized for work not done or for non-conformance to the requirements of the contract. The deduction formula for the various services provided a computed deduction sum which was to be deducted from the agreed lump-sum amount given to the contractor for their monthly progressive payment. Thus, records of work done or not done had to be documented properly. These records were entered in the centralized management information system (CMIS). Every day, hospital staff and CC personnel would log in to the CMIS to access the various work orders, inspections, etc.

Hence, it can be seen that all personnel involved in this project had to learn not only how to manage the contract but also all of the intricacies and requirements associated with the contract. At the commencement of the contract, appropriate experienced personnel were lacking. Some did not understand the contract requirements well, which led to overclaims by the contractor in some instances or to unreasonable deductions made by the hospital staff.

One of the ways that MOH decided to resolve the disputes during the validation meetings was to employ a middleman to mediate between the two parties of the contract. For this, SIHAT was appointed to participate in the validation meetings and to monitor the works and performance of the contractors. This assisted in lessening the number of disputes that arose in the validation meetings.

The key to resolving the CCs' manpower needs was training. The CCs had embarked on programmes throughout the years to train their personnel in the management, supervision, and administration of the works. Where works required on-job training, such training was organized to train the technicians and workers to be competent in their field of work. Training sessions were conducted not only within the CCs for staff and workers, but also for hospital staff to understand the requirements of the contract. Only in the area of specialized engineering did the CCs need further improvement. This was provided by way of advance training for the key engineers and technicians, which addressed the shortage of such personnel on account of resignations and redeployments. By the end of the concession period, the CCs had developed the expertise, knowledge, and experience to ensure that the management and maintenance of hospital support services was up to standard.

The essence of recruiting and retaining qualified and competent technical personnel and engineers was to ensure that their competency and professionalism were on par with that of other clinical professionals. It is mandatory that clinical professionals be registered with the respective professional bodies and undergo continuous professional development. However, this was not the case with the hospitals' engineering and facility professionals. Many hospitals often employ a chargeman instead of a biomedical engineer to oversee the medical equipment. Thus, continuous training of technicians and engineers should be the norm to ensure that HSS quality standards are maintained.

## 6.2.2. Hospital and Departmental Expansion and Upgrading

At the commencement of the project, there were 127 hospitals for the contract. At the end, there were 148 hospitals, indicating an increase of 22 hospitals.

This increase stretched the manpower and resource capabilities of the CCs as they sought to accommodate the broader scope of responsibilities. In addition, new extensions to current facilities, the upgrading of existing facilities and equipment to higher capacities, and new installations within current facilities added demands on the contract. An increase in patient population and the number of beds also added demands, straining the clinical services and support services provided by the hospitals and the CCs respectively. This increase in demand on account of patient population can be attributed to the increase in population of the country and to the government's better healthcare provision.

The stress and strains attributable to the demands posed by utility and support services demands in adopting the healthcare service provided by the government was continuous throughout the period of the contract and was never adequately or sufficiently resolved. Measures to resolve one part led to more unresolved parts, which were left uncovered because of the complexity of the healthcare services and changing technology. For example, electrical demands may be adequately planned for new hospitals but may not be adequate for the subsequent expansion of the hospital. Even beds for wards suffered the same consequence. Some hospitals had to locate beds along corridors. Delays in operations were common in many hospitals, due not only to an inadequate number of surgeons but also to an inadequate number of operating theatres.

Many new projects planned by the Ministry of Health were not communicated to or coordinated with the CCs. Thus, when a CC was planning for an extension or new equipment installation, it gave no consideration to the extra demand on utilities, which resulted in an inadequate supply of electricity and water. Some projects were delayed because the hospital's electrical system reached its maximum capacity. New cables and transformers had to be laid and installed for the extensions. An adequate and continuous electricity supply is considered critical for a hospital, as a non-supply would lead to the failure of critical life support equipment within the hospital. Such a failure could lead to patient death.

Throughout the largest period of the contract, there was no central coordinating body within most hospitals to oversee energy and other utility demands. The discovery of this inadequacy was recognized towards the end of the contract period, when some form of a system for checking energy and other utilities was adopted by the MOH and the CCs to address the issue. This somewhat improved on the inadequacy.

Water supply to most hospitals, except during times of non-supply (such as when a pipe was broken) was generally satisfactory. The general issue relating to water supply was the adequacy of the forty-eight hours' storage capacity within the hospital compound. The idea of forty-eight hours' storage capacity is that there is sufficient water supply within the hospital compound to cover a short-term emergency water supply shortage. Causes of a water supply shortage could be broken main pipes, no supply from the municipal mains, and major drought. It was found that most hospitals did not have adequate forty-eight hours' storage capacity. Some had a capacity of less than twenty-four hours. Since the discovery of this inadequacy, measures were taken by the MOH to improve on the capacities. Municipalities assisted by ensuring that sufficient water supply would reach the hospitals first in times of shortage and drought.

One reason that equipment might be upgraded is that the equipment is old, has reached the end of its life, and needs to be replaced with new and more-advanced equipment. At times, because of poor maintenance of equipment, equipment might be replaced before it has reached its life expectancy. This was not uncommon in the management of the project.

The upgrading and extension of the hospital is a continuous process for every hospital's administrative body. A hospital may be upgraded or expanded because of improvements in, changes to, and/or development of new medical technology or medical management methodology. The discovery of new methods of diagnosis and treatment will lead to new facilities being built to cater to the new developments. Demands for better patient care increase the need to build new facilities in current hospitals which had not been originally planned. Old departments are replaced by new departments that use new technology and methodologies. Even human resources need to be retrained or recruited to cater to the new developments. When space becomes a constraint within current hospital compounds, new hospitals will be built. All of these things will cause strains to the existing utilities and infrastructure. Good hospital administrators are needed to make plans for this inevitability, all for the delivery of good patient care to the community.

## 6.2.3. CMIS

The centralized management information system (CMIS) that was developed tremendously assisted the MOH, the hospitals, and the CCs in disseminating information and managing the hospital support services. However, there were shortcomings in its implementation.

Firstly, accurate and timely data entry had to be implemented diligently by the CCs. Occasionally, errors were made in the data entries. This led to erroneous interpretation and analysis, and non-attendance to the issues at hand. Late data entries resulted in late reporting and late follow-up actions.

Information pertaining to the asset register was found to be inadequate and erroneous. For example, three chillers were located at a site, but the asset register recorded only two chillers. Capacities were not recorded for each asset, which prevented the CMIS users from determining the size of the asset, be it a water tank, a water pump, an air-conditioning unit, and so forth. The basic information about any asset should, as much as possible, include asset number, manufacturer, model, serial number, asset name, purchase cost, date of supply, department, location, condition, warranty expiry date, etc. This information was not found in all of the asset registers. Assets in the asset register, especially biomedical equipment, were also found to be erroneously ascribed to another category. Thus, data entry clerks who are responsible for the asset register need to be trained to place assets in the correct asset category.

The CMIS captured with fair accuracy the work orders, whether scheduled or unscheduled, and the reports that were produced were generally fair and up to date. Concerns arose for work orders that took a long time – six months or more – to be addressed and then closed. Another concerns was that there were frequent breakdowns of information about plant rooms, as the information was not captured in the system. With this breakdown of information, the CC could not report with any degree of accuracy that equipment in the plant rooms was due for replacement. There were times when the information about the equipment faults was sketchy, was unreliable, and did not reflect the true nature of the fault. And resolutions of faults were not recorded in many cases. The reason for the plant rooms failing to report faults in the system might be that there was less reporting by the CCs via work requests, as there were no penalties for non-reporting. Where there was more interaction with the users, there were many users reporting, and thus the CCs focused their attention on these areas. Examples of this are the fusing of light bulbs in user areas, leaks in pipes and ceilings, breakdowns of user equipments especially biomedical equipment, etc.

## 6.2.4. Deductions

The deduction process that was developed was complicated and thus easily subject to computational errors by various parties, including the hospitals and the CCs. Both the personnel from the hospitals and the CCs need to understand thoroughly the mechanism of the deduction process and the deduction formulas. They also need to understand the importance of being timely when applying the deduction process to the chain of activities in all five hospital support services. A hospital's failure to apply the deduction amount could lead to a loss of opportunity to penalize the CCs for non-performance or non-conformance regarding the works under the contract. The overdeduction of payment amounts meant a loss of revenue for the CCs. Thus all activities and amounts for deduction have to be scrutinized in a fair and just manner to minimize disputes.

For facility engineering maintenance services (FEMS) and biomedical engineering maintenance services (BEMS), the non-performance or non-conformance of activities related to the TRPI needs to be constantly monitored and supervised by diligent hospital staff and also by personnel from the monitoring consultant, SIHAT. The non-conformance of scheduled activities like planned preventive maintenance (PPM) can be captured by CMIS, but unscheduled activities and work orders need to be properly recorded if they are to be captured. Because of this weakness in the system, especially where there was less supervision by the hospital, such as in plant rooms, the non-performance of activities was relatively high and the CCs escaped non-performance deductions. Normally, the CC would rectify the problem before the problem (such as a breakdown) came to light, especially for those non-conformance activities as required in the TRPI.

In wards, this abuse of the system would be unlikely occur, as the ward staff would have sent a work request to the CMIS for something such as the replacement of fused light bulbs. Another weakness was the warranty management for new equipment, a process which was poorly supervised and neglected by the CCs because they believe that the duty of maintenance of new equipment fell on the vendors or contractors. No deductions were made on the CCs for unsatisfactory warranty management.

For linen laundry services (LLS) and clinical waste management services (CWMS), payment was made according to weight, and there could be errors in the weights recorded. The procedure was to have hospital personnel witness the weighing. Lazy hospital staff might leave the whole process of weighing to the CC staff, opening up the possibility of malpractice by overweighing the linen or waste in order to claim more.

In many cases, after the validation process and the application of a deduction for non-performance and non-conformance, it was found that the total deduction amounts were small, perhaps less than 5 per cent of the total concession company contract fee for the month. On many occasions when the deduction amount was this small, the CCs opted to receive a deduction rather than perform the activity. The deduction process was thus rendered ineffective in many situations covered by the contract.

## 6.2.5. HSIP

An HSIP was prepared so that the hospitals and the CCs could make reference to the responsibilities of the various parties named in the contract, the schedule and timeline for each party to fulfil its obligations, and the list of standards, procedures, and policies to follow. The document was specific to each hospital, as it would be too bulky and impractical to produce a single overall document to cover all hospitals.

The documents were usually prepared one or two months before the end of each calendar year. However, this deadline was not met by many hospitals, which resulted in delays in approving the document. The delay could be attributed to corrections, disagreements about the draft, or the large workload of the hospital directors. Mistakes and errors might be found in the yearly document, such as the list of replacement staff not being updated or the schedule for the inspection of PPM not being updated and being made impractical to carry out. Sometimes the hospital staff disagreed about the schedule of visits and inspections proposed by the CCs, so the schedule required adjustments and corrections. Hospital directors are busy people, as they attend many meetings and functions and perform many activities, so they sometimes delayed their review of the HSIP or overlooked it altogether. The delays were mitigated by preparing the documents earlier than the norm of one to two months in advance, and approving the documents in January of the following year. One of the areas of disagreement may have been due to the CCs not providing sufficient data or information to the hospitals for checking and vetting. Changes in both the hospital's and CC's organizational structure might also lead to delays in the approval process.

Whilst the hospitals and the CCs made efforts to produce the "perfect" document for the HSIP, it was usually found that the documents were never adequate or complete. The inadequacies included incomplete or late information on asset listings, PPM schedules, staff replacements, contact personnel in the event of emergencies, procedures, contingency plans, layout plans, exemption lists, BER (beyond economic repair) equipment, lists of cleaning chemicals for cleaning, etc. Fortunately, the documents were dynamic, so any changes made during the year could still be incorporated within the year.

Layout plans were of particular concern, as many hospitals had no technical plans for reference. This affected maintenance works. The physical presence of utilities and the technical details of civil structures and mechanical and electrical installations made things difficult. Most of the time, maintenance personnel carried out their works on assumptions and guesswork. For those hospitals that had technical plans, little attempt had been made to update the drawings to reflect the latest changes on the ground.

The contingency plans for emergencies listed in the HSIP were inadequate, poorly prepared, or non-existent. Contingency plans are important in the event of, say, a loss of power, where the generator(s) can supply a sufficient amount of electricity. A flood or a fire can also disrupt a hospital's services, so contingency plans are important to have for such situations.

Audits carried out by the monitoring consultant, SIHAT, usually highlighted the inadequacy of the HSIP given the factors described above. Improvements were made in some hospitals, but these were never complete. As some of the aspects in the HSIP were not critical or important, these were waived or ignored by both the hospitals and the CCs when approving the document.

## 6.2.6. Third-Party Clause

Implementation of the third-party clause was easier said than done, the reason being that permission had to be granted by the CCs and the clauses were to be applied only in exceptional cases. Every avenue had to be explored by the CCs first before alternative measures would be considered. However, as time could be of the essence, the CCs could not take too long to find a third party to undertake the service. There were times when the hospital took the initiative to find a third party to carry out the service with the consent of the CCs during emergencies, especially for critical medical cases. No time charges could be immediately determined for such cases.

Sometimes finding alternative hospitals for the immediate diagnosis and/or treatment of a patient was not possible, so the hospital would send the patient, usually by ambulance, to a hospital in another state or to a regional hospital several tens of kilometres away.

For cases where time was not of the essence, including breakdowns of a less critical facility, or a biomedical facility such as a CT scan room, time could be taken to find the best cost for the alternative solution. A formalized terms of agreement could then be worked out between the parties.

## 6.2.7. Reimbursable Works

The reimbursable works supplementary agreement, which was introduced in January 2003, led to less confusion about works that were classified as maintainable and works that were in addition to the contract. Maintainable works were non-chargeable as they were deemed to be included in the original contract. Reimbursable works were chargeable as variation works. For example, small touch-ups of paint were maintenance related and therefore were not chargeable. However, if there was a need to repaint an entire wall, then this was considered to fall under the reimbursable scope of works and was therefore chargeable as a variation works.

Items that were old and obsolete, damaged, vandalized, or missing could be considered as reimbursable works so long as the approval was given by the hospital. To effectively administer a reimbursable works item, a protocol had to be established between the hospital and the CC to avoid disputes. Hospitals were at liberty to choose their own vendors or contractors to reconstruct or replace the damaged or missing items. If other vendors or contractors were chosen by the hospital to undertake the same reimbursable works, then the CCs would be paid a nominal fee for attending to the carrying out of coordination works.

Involving the CCs in the reimbursable works meant that the CCs were entrusted with a great responsibility to ensure that the reimbursable works were completed to the satisfaction of the hospital and were up to good quality standards.

## 6.2.8. Quality Assurance Programme

The quality assurance programme (QAP) as required in the contract was not implemented immediately upon the signing of the project. Instead, it took many years of discussions, pilot studies, and projects before the proper implementation took place, which was in 2006. Even then only certain items were selected for implementation. The reasons are as stated in section 2.8 of this book – the inherent difficulties of the contract and a lack of information.

The basis of the QAP was that the CCs would meet the quality requirements of ISO 9001:2008 and the earlier ISO version on quality. CCs were non-enthusiastic about implementing the QAP because any non-compliance regarding QAP targets did not result in a deduction of fees. Fees were only deducted for non-implementation of the QAP and non-submission of QAP reports.

The system that was set up for the QAP was acceptable within the ambit of the contract. The indicators and standards promulgated were acceptable, although not all of them were implemented. The process for verification of the QAP was adequately covered, although with many layers, which made it complicated and subject to errors when determining the accuracy and completeness of records and data. Data verification officers (DVOs) had to be very conversant with the process to avoid mistakes, errors, and disputes. Thus the implementation was considered by many stakeholders of the contract to be an exercise in futility.

However, this exercise, although not fee-deductible, led the CCs to strive for better quality in the hospital support services. At the very least, there were measurable items for the CCs to base their progress on. It is for this reason that the purpose of the QAP is seen as having been fulfilled.

## 6.2.9. FEMS and BEMS

The International Facilities Management Association (IFMA) defines facilities management as a profession that encompasses multiple disciplines to ensure functionality of the built environment by integrating people, place, process, and technology. The key component is the built environment. That is, whatever is constructed, installed, and fitted is to be managed in such a manner that its functionality serves its intended purposes. IFMA espouses eleven core competencies, namely communication; emergency and preparedness and business continuity; environmental stewardship and sustainability; finance and business; human factors; leadership and strategy; operations and maintenance; project management; quality; real estate and property management; and technology.

As can be seen, facility management is highly complex. It is even more complex in the hospital or healthcare environment, where patient care is of the utmost priority. The facility management of the MOH hospitals that was practised in the privatization programme did not apply all the core competencies recommended under the IFMA 2006. For example, as the MOH hospitals were government properties, real estate and property management was not applicable. Finance and business was equally not applicable. The major competencies that were applied were operations and maintenance, project management, communications, emergency preparedness, environmental stewardship and sustainability, leadership and strategy, and technology.

All the facilities and buildings need to be designed according to patient flow, criticality of the service, and clinical requirements. The support services systems, such as the system for medical gases, the pneumatic transfer system, a critical and uninterrupted power supply, and air conditioning and mechanical ventilation, have to be designed according to the standards and clinical requirements.

FEMS is only one of the important components of facility management. It is concerned mainly with the operations and maintenance of the critical engineering system supporting the healthcare facility. Thus, the concession agreement (CA), through the TRPI and the MAP, was scripted to reflect this.

Maintenance management by the CCs was generally well organized, with a single facility organizational structure under a single facility manager at each hospital. These were then divided into functional departments depending on the size of the hospital. For the bigger hospitals, functional departments include the mechanical, electrical, civil, biomedical, housekeeping, and administration disciplines. Smaller hospitals have combinations of the services. For specialty works, the regional offices of the CCs gave support to the hospitals upon request. One of the CCs had a variant in the organizational structure, parcelling out the services to subcontractors under the five support services of FEMS, BEMS, CLS, LLS, and CWMS but having one facility manager control all of these.

The general best practices of maintenance were followed throughout the duration of the contract for both planned and unplanned activities. Planned preventive maintenance was generally in accord with the schedule, although there were misses (albeit minimal ones). CCs made good attempts to comply with statutory standards and ensure that all licenses were renewed before the due dates.

Breakdown maintenance was mainly unscheduled or else followed from PPM inspection as corrective maintenance with a fourteen-day window period for rectification or repair. Predictive maintenance or condition-based monitoring maintenance was not practised widely throughout the concession period because there was no such requirement in the contract. Nevertheless, the CCs implemented some form of predictive maintenance practice using thermograph, oil analysis, and the AC monitors at newly installed chiller plants.

The CCs together with MOH and SIHAT developed hospital engineering planned preventive maintenance (HEPPM) checklists for all the equipment belonging both to the facility and biomedical engineering. These checklists were based on the manufacturers' recommendations and industrial best practices. This assisted the engineers and technicians to check and troubleshoot problems, defects, and issues related to equipment during the inspection tours.

Works orders generated from the CMIS for both planned and unplanned activities were generally followed and attended to. The high uptime target reflected this in the CMIS. There were instances of delay in the closing of work orders on account of many reasons, such no spare parts, delay in finding spare parts, no availability of spare parts due to obsolescence, etc. Occasionally, a delay was caused by an incompetent technician who could not resolve the engineering problem and left the issue dangling until a more competent technician arrived at the site of trouble.

The CMIS was used to track and analyse work orders and records of PPM done within the fourteen-day window and after fourteen days' duration. Long delays beyond fourteen days were captured and reported in the CMIS. This was useful for identifying the long delays, as delays might be due to many reasons. Most pertinent delays in resolving equipment breakdowns were on account of the unavailability of spare parts, particularly for old and obsolete equipment whose manufacturer no longer existed and, thus, for which the spare part was no longer available. In such a situation, the hospital may have to look for a replacement, which may be very costly.

Changes in the function of the departments could cause problems and disruption to services in the hospitals. The CCs had to be kept informed of the changes so as to make adjustments in the administration of the FEMS and BEMS so that those services did not suffer. In many cases, the coordinated changes did not occur, which resulted in the need to use corridors as rooms or wards.

Safety awareness regarding FEMS in most hospitals was generally poor and inadequate. No safety manual was created for any of the hospitals, and no safety committees were formed or constituted. Thus, compliance with the Occupational and Safety Health Act was considered inadequate in most cases. The hospitals left much room for improvement.

## 6.2.10. CWMS

The practice of CWMS by both hospitals and CCs was considered excellent by the World Health Organization (WHO) on account of the stringent measures that were implemented and enforced by the MOH and the Department of Environment (DOE). The WHO concluded that the CWMS was of a high international standard. Despite this, there were areas of shortfalls during the contract's implementation stage. Among these was the breakdown of the clinical waste incinerators at the centralized incineration plants, which affected the rate of incineration and caused backlogs of clinical waste. The CCs' contingency plan was to store the clinical waste in refrigerated containers. However, this measure was inadequate, as the risk of disease outbreaks loomed high. Because of this, the government of Malaysia, under MOH, took control of the situation by calling other incinerators to assist in incinerating the backlogs of clinical waste from one of the CCs. From the experience of the backlog incident, it was seen that extra capacity for clinical waste at incineration plants needed to be installed. It was also determined that proper maintenance of plants should be practised.

Another area of shortfall was the inadequate storage space for clinical waste in hospital storerooms or storehouses, especially during peak loads. This might have been due to the expansion of the hospital, with an increase in the number of beds, without allowing for an expansion of the clinical waste store. Occasionally, collection of clinical waste was delayed, leading to a backlog in the storerooms.

Another incident of minor non-compliance in clinical practice was the incidence of sharps injuries as a result of worker carelessness in the handling of the sharps containers.

Mixing of general waste bags and clinical waste bags was found on several occasions during inspections. Containers and bags filled beyond three quarters limits (the maximum permitted by the contract) were also detected.

To overcome these problems, hospital staff and CC workers underwent proper training to learn the proper procedures for handling clinical waste.

## 6.2.11. Cleansing

Cleaning service standards provided by the CCs were generally acceptable and good, as they met most of the requirements set out in the TRPI and MAP.

One major issue was the inexperience of the workers and supervisors, as there was a constant turnover of cleansing workers in the hospitals. Continuous training of new workers at hospitals ensured that the cleansing services did not suffer. Communication with the workers was an issue at some hospitals, as the

CCs employed foreign (immigrant) workers who did not understand the local language and customs.

Non-conformance issues related to cleansing included the wrong use of coloured mops for various purposes and the failure to follow cleansing procedures.

## 6.2.12. LLS

The CCs' delivery service of linens to hospitals was generally considered adequate and timely. There were not many complaints from the hospitals of shortfalls in the supply of linens. However, quality was merely satisfactory, as there were defects to the linens, which required frequent repairs and replacement. Quality controls ensured that the good linen was passed through to minimize defective linens.

Linens were generally stored at the central store upon delivery to the hospitals and were then delivered to satellite stores within the hospital.

There were cases when the weighing of linen was done without hospital staff being present. This sometimes led to malpractice, namely the falsifying of soiled linen weights to pad up results.

Linen were cleaned at central laundry facilities using the most advanced laundry technology, which included continuous batch washers (CBWs) or tunnel washers, automated ironers, and folders. These facilities ensured the quality of the linen and were able to meet the linen-supply demand.

## 6.2.13. SIHAT

SIHAT was appointed basically, as the monitoring consultant for the contract to monitor the performance of the CCs. Its other key roles were to be the professional advisor and consultant for MOH with respect to hospital support services, minor works, and radiology equipment.

However, as the geographical area was wide, including the whole of Malaysia, SIHAT could not deploy one consultant to each hospital on account of its limited personnel. Therefore, monitoring consultants were organized so that monitoring of the smaller district hospitals was done by grouping these hospitals into clusters of two or three per consultant.

The experience and competency of the monitoring consultant was essential if he or she were to effectively monitor the performance of the CCs. SIHAT conducted training for its consultants twice yearly, wherein new recruits were trained and current employees received an update on the methodology of monitoring the CCs. In addition, the zone managers played an important role in guiding the consultants to grasp the right procedures, requirements, and management of the contract. Difficult disputes were usually addressed by the zone managers. In many cases, SIHAT acted as mediator and quasi arbitrator when there were disputes between the hospitals and the CCs, especially at meetings to validate deductions.

Besides monitoring the CCs, SIHAT conducted other assessments of the CCs on a periodic basis. These assessments included the semi-annual contractor performance assessments (CPAs), six objective assessments (OA) of selected hospitals done yearly, six equipment assessments (EA) carried out per annum, and an occasional condition assessment of equipment or system as requested by MOH. Reports submitted for these assessments were very much appreciated by MOH, as they gave a realistic independent assessment of the CCs' performance. The reports included not only the shortcomings of the CCs but also areas of improvement for the CCs and the hospitals. The assessments also assisted the MOH in identifying equipment that needed to be replaced, particularly equipment which was aged and obsolete.

## 6.3. Conclusion

Hospital equipment and facilities are constantly changing as a result of expansion of services, new equipment and technology, new standards, rules, and regulations, and the obsolescence of equipment that needs to be upgraded. Although it may be easy to replace mobile equipment, larger, static equipment, such as MRI machines, CT machines, or tomotherapy machines, is harder to replace, as these machines require a properly designed technical room and support utilities.

Most hospitals in the country are headed by either doctors or accountants. Whilst the doctor is good at understanding the hospital's service requirements, and whilst the accountant is good at understanding the hospital's financial requirements, there is also a need to ensure that hospital assets are taken care of. Many hospitals, particularly those in a Third World country like Malaysia, however, do not have professional engineers who specialize in healthcare operations and who can assist the hospital in matching the facility's requirements with the service requirements and ultimately meet financial requirements. Hospitals on many occasions engage consulting architects and engineers who just look after the development in isolation and do not have a long-term strategic master plan for hospital development. Even in this area, the country's short supply of professional engineers with a background in the medical field has a bearing on the type of advice offered for the proper planning and design of hospital and healthcare facilities.

It is important to note that asset creation has a significant impact on the operation and maintenance cost of the equipment. The accountants normally focus on the capital expenditure requirements for acquiring the asset and its financial return for the year. Thus, it is the engineer's duty to guide the accountant on the operating cost so that the overall cost of owning the asset can be ascertained. Without this type of guidance, a hospital may buy cheap machines and end up with expensive maintenance and repair bills. It could be a case of being penny wise and pound foolish. Hence, it is important for a hospital to adopt a long-term strategy for asset management to avoid service interruption or, worse, jeopardize patients' safety and health.

The Ministry of Health, Malaysia, took the right steps in privatizing the hospital support systems for five services, as these areas were out of the ambit and specialized areas of doctors and hospital administrators in the late 1990s (see the reasons as given in Section 1.2). The decision led to tremendous improvement in the healthcare services provided by the government of Malaysia through the MOH. This bold decision led to the upgrade and improvement of healthcare services throughout the country. The steps taken enabled the upgrading of workers' skills and quality in providing support services to healthcare facilities in the country, especially the technical personnel and engineers. This HSS implementation can be attributed to the many decision makers, implementers, staff members, and workers of the hospitals and CCs, and to the many consultants, vendors, and contractors who diligently and dedicatedly contributed their efforts to the project's success. The understanding and cooperation between the hospitals, the CCs, the monitoring consultant SIHAT, and the MOH was indeed exemplary for a contract of this nature. Disputes, especially regarding deductions for payments, did arise, but at the end of the day these were resolved by all parties for the sake of the service and better patient care.

Still, as is the case when any new system is introduced, there were hiccups experienced in the implementation of the HSS system in the hospitals. Over time, these were resolved through experience, understanding, sound-minded engagement, meetings, and resolutions.

The success of this HSS system has become a model for other government departments to emulate. The private sector healthcare industry, which includes private hospitals and medical centres, has also emulated this HSS system. The results of the implementation of the HSS can be seen in the many international standards being upheld by the practitioners in the industry, such as the clinical waste management system and the linen and laundry service system. Facilities engineering maintenance services and biomedical engineering maintenance services adopted international standards of maintenance using a well-established central management monitoring system and also adopted the international nomenclature standards for categorizing hospital assets.

The privatization of the HSS has contributed to the creation and development of a core of specialist hospital engineers and medical technicians who have the necessary knowledge and experience to operate and maintain the hospital equipment effectively. This, however, does not fully address the shortage of trained and experienced engineers with hospital experience, but at the very least a pool of experts are in existence to cater to the medical industry. With the implementation of the Medical Device Act 2012 in Malaysia, there is a pressing need for practitioners and engineers to equip themselves with the relevant engineering knowledge of and experience with all of the facility and biomedical engineering equipment and devices within the healthcare facilities.

Notwithstanding the hiccups faced by the implementers of the privatized hospital support services, the successful implementation of the HSS systems for all government hospitals and healthcare institutions has enabled the government of Malaysia to decide to continue with the system – with improvements - for the future.

# Appendix

# Technical Requirements and Performance Indicators (TRPI)[7]

<table>
<tr><td colspan="4">Facility Engineering Maintenance Services (FEMS)</td></tr>
<tr><th>Item</th><th>Scope of work</th><th>Requirement</th><th>Indicators</th></tr>
<tr>
<td>1.1</td>
<td>Maintain all facilities, including civil engineering works, mechanical and electrical (M&E) systems, and plant and non-medical equipment<br><br>a) Carry out routine inspections, and preventive and corrective maintenance<br>b) Carry out other FEMS-related activities</td>
<td>a) All relevant Malaysian statutory requirements<br>b) All relevant Standards and Industrial Research Institute of Malaysia (SIRIM) codes of practice and standards<br>c) All recommendations from the relevant manufacturers<br>d) General requirements in civil and M&E engineering in facility engineering preventive maintenance requirements by the government of Malaysia<br>e) Uptime targets<br>f) Response times</td>
<td>a) Uptimes<br>b) Response times<br>c) Number and frequency of breakdowns<br>d) Number and frequency of each category of non-compliance relating to service requirements and standards, as follows:<br><br>i. Failure to perform any scheduled maintenance task<br>ii. Failure to perform any scheduled maintenance task on time</td>
</tr>
</table>

7    Source: Concession Agreement with Government of Malaysia and Companies 1996

| | | | |
|---|---|---|---|
| | c) Provide all personnel, tools, instruments, spare parts, materials, transportation, workshops, and facilities, and anything else necessary to carry out maintenance <br> d) Arrange and verify warranty maintenance carried out by others <br> e) Provide technical advice on facility maintenance | g) All spare parts shall be new and unused genuine parts from equipment manufacturers or acceptable equivalents <br> h) All materials shall be new, of approved standards, and compatible with existing materials <br> i) All workmanship shall be in accordance with approved codes and good engineering practices | iii. Failure to achieve any equipment uptime target <br> iv. Non-compliance with any relevant Malaysian statutory requirement or standard <br> v. All other non-compliance of requirements as stipulated in the contract |
| 1.2 | Operate all engineering plants and installations <br><br> a) Provide all necessary personnel (including electrical chargemen, boilermen, and visiting engineers) <br> b) Maintain daily operation log sheets <br> c) Provide everything necessary to carry out the operational service except for the supply of electricity, fuel, medical, gases and other public utilities <br> d) Provide technical advice on the operation of engineering equipment, plant, and installations, including energy management | a) All relevant Malaysian statutory requirements <br> b) All relevant SIRIM codes of practice <br> c) All recommendations from the relevant equipment manufacturers <br> d) Valid certificates of fitness and licenses at all times <br> e) Operate with optimum efficiency at agreed parameters | a) Number of violations of law <br> b) Number of accidents <br> c) Operating efficiencies <br> d) Number and frequency of each category of non-compliance with service requirements and standards, as follows: <br><br> i. Failure to comply with any relevant Malaysian statutory requirement or Standards and Industrial Research Institute of Malaysia (SIRIM) code of practice <br> ii. Failure to achieve any agreed operating efficiency |

| 1.3 | Provide technical advice on reimbursable works, and carry out the reimbursable works if approved | In accord with good engineering practices | Non-compliance of requirements shall constitute a very serious non-conformance to service standards infraction |
|---|---|---|---|
| 1.4 | Testing and commissioning of equipment, reimbursable works, and development projects by others | a) Witness and submit observations and comments <br> b) Include relevant data in MIS | -ditto- |
| 1.5 | Provide, implement, and maintain a computerized management information system (MIS) | a) Submit MIS for approval <br> b) Comply with MIS requirements in the contract | -ditto- |
| 1.6 | Establish and implement a fault-reporting, requisition, and feedback system | Submit the system for approval | -ditto- |
| 1.7 | Institute and maintain a documented quality assurance programme (QAP) | Prepare and submit QAP for approval | -ditto- |
| 1.8 | Prepare and submit maintenance and QAP reports | a) Submit together with claims for payment (but not less frequent than once every three months), which include a summary of maintenance service performed, uptime targets achieved, analysis of deficiencies, and recommendations | -ditto- |

| | | | |
|---|---|---|---|
| 1.9 | a) Provide demonstrations and training for users and operators on the safe and correct use of engineering facilities, as well as user maintenance<br>b) Conduct fire drills and provide demonstrations on fire safety | At least once a year | -ditto- |
| 1.10 | Maintain adequately staffed and equipped workshop in contract hospitals (on-site) | a) May utilize existing workshop spaces where available; otherwise, construct new workshops on-site at own cost<br>b) Pay for utilities tapped from the contract hospitals | -ditto- |
| 1.11 | Take over all existing operating and maintenance manuals and drawings:<br><br>a) Set up and maintain library for technical documents<br>b) Procure necessary technical documents from manufacturers and former project consultants, where available | a) Procure all necessary documents where available<br>b) Computerize all site plans, architectural drawings, and service drawings relevant to maintenance and operation | -ditto- |
| 1.12 | Take over all existing spare parts, engineering and building materials, tools, and instruments | Purchase based on rates to be determined by Government Valuation Department | |

| | | | |
|---|---|---|---|
| 1.13 | Indemnify the government against any claims for damages to property and injuries to any member of the public, contract hospital staff, or concession company (CC) staff arising from negligence on the part of the CC in carrying out the work | | |

| Biomedical Engineering Maintenance Services (BEMS) | | | |
|---|---|---|---|
| **Item** | **Scope of work** | **Requirement** | **Indicators** |
| 2.1 | To carry out a comprehensive programme of planed and scheduled maintenance for all medical and laboratory equipment

To provide effective and responsive repair on all medical equipment, and provision of on-call and emergency staff

To carry out acceptance testing as well as safety and performance tests on all incoming new equipment | a) All relevant Malaysian statutory regulations
b) All recommendations from manufacturers are to be followed and will supersede the documents in (*b*) and (*c*), below
c) General requirements as indicated in the latest edition of the ECRI publication *Procedures for Inspection and Preventive Maintenance Manual* are to be followed
d) For equipment without a manufacturer's manual and for which no manual is available in item 3, the procedures from the latest edition of the *Medical Equipment Management in Hospitals* by the American Society for Hospital Engineering are to be followed
e) All safety requirements as stated in the IEC 601 and collaterals, MS 838 for radiological equipment, and relevant standards for nuclear and radiotherapy equipment
f) At least two hours on-site response time for repair calls, and not exceeding fifteen minutes' on-site response time for emergency calls
g) Twenty-four-hour on-call basis | a) Total preventive maintenance schedule (monthly)
b) Outstanding preventive maintenance (backlog)
c) Response time
d) Number of emergency calls attended
e) Number of safety tests and safety checks performed per year

Note:
i. Failure to perform PPM shall constitute a very serious non-conformance to service standard infraction
ii. Failure to respond within the stipulated time frame shall constitute a very serious non-conformance infraction
iii. Failure to perform safety tests and safety checks shall constitute a very serious non-conformance infraction |

| | | | |
|---|---|---|---|
| | | h) Calibration, functional checks, and safety checks according to the manufacturer's recommendation shall be conducted after each repair works<br>i) Guideline on acceptance testing and on service testing of medical equipment, MOH | iv. Non-conformance to legal requirement shall constitute a very serious non-conformance infraction |
| 2.2 | To provide mechanisms to avoid failure or breakdown during diagnosis and therapy | Implement a mechanism to avoid failure or breakdown during use | a) Percent uptime<br>b) Number of occurrences or breakdowns during procedure or use<br><br>Note:<br>i. Non-implementation of the contingency plan is a very serious non-conformance infraction<br>ii. Service disruption due to failure of biomedical engineering maintenance services shall constitute a very serious non-conformance infraction |
| 2.3 | To carry out all works necessary to provide an uptime guarantee on maintenance uptime | a) Critical (including life support):<br>• 99% equipment uptime < 5 years<br>• 95% equipment uptime 5–10 years | a) % uptime<br>b) Uptime guarantee |

| | | | |
|---|---|---|---|
| | | • 90% service uptime for common functional units<br>b) Patient support machines:<br>• 96% equipment uptime < 5 years<br>• 92% equipment uptime 5–10 years<br>• 80% service uptime for common functional unit<br>c) Reimbursement for failing to meet uptime | Note:<br>i. Not maintaining uptime target is an extremely serious non-conformance infraction |
| 2.4 | To implement the hospital engineering quality assurance programme | a) Quality assurance programme, MOH<br>b) Attain ISO standards within five years | a) Implementation of the programme<br>b) ISO certification<br><br>Note:<br>i. Non-updating of computerized documentation is a serious non-conformance infraction<br>ii. Falsification of computerized documentation is an extremely serious non-conformance infraction |
| 2.5 | To establish a computerized documentation system, which shall include equipment control records and a computerized counterpart | a) Associated basic modules for maintenance management work, i.e. work order, asset register, stock control, budgetary control, preventive maintenance<br>b) Treasury's inventory log cards | a) Equipment inventory updated semi-annually<br>b) Number of pieces of equipment tagged and entered in inventory<br>c) Number of warranty notifications |

| | | | |
|---|---|---|---|
| | To provide quarterly reports on maintenance activities to MOH and the hospital administration<br><br>To notify departments of warranty expiration | | Note:<br>  i. Non-dating of computerized documentation is a serious non-conformance infraction<br> ii. Falsification of computerized documentation is an extremely serious non-conformance infraction |
| 2.6 | To dispose of/ remove unwanted medical equipment | Guidelines on disposing of equipment limited to transportation to condemn store within the MOH's hospital or institution | Number of pieces of equipment disposed of according to MOH guidelines |
| 2.7 | To implement procedures for dealing with hazardous matter and handling contaminated equipment | MOH standard requirements and standards in dealing with hazardous matter and handling contaminated equipment | Number of hazardous works carried out according to procedures by the consortium<br><br>Note:<br>Failing to implement the procedure for dealing with hazardous matter shall constitute a serious non-conformance infraction |
| 2.8 | To cooperate in the investigation of related incidents | Produce report on the status of the maintenance history of the equipment | Number of reported equipment-related incidents<br><br>Note:<br>Failure to submit report as required shall constitute non-conformance |

| 2.9 | To train users on the daily user maintenance procedure (excludes clinical procedure related to the equipment) | Identify the need for training on specific medical equipment and the action taken | Number of user training sessions conducted<br><br>Note:<br>Failing to carry out user training shall constitute an extreme serious non-conformance infraction |
|---|---|---|---|
| 2.10 | To maintain a stock of genuine spares | a) To assist in maintaining the uptime targets<br>b) Ensuring an adequate supply of maintenance kits | Availability of critical and recommended spares<br><br>Note:<br>Not maintaining the genuine spares or the manufacturer's recommended spare shall constitute a serious non-conformance infraction |
| 2.11 | Establish a library of user and service manuals | All biomedical engineering workshops shall have a documented list of service manuals | Number of service manuals not available for critical-care equipment |

| | Cleansing (CLS) | | |
|---|---|---|---|
| **Item** | **Scope of work** | **Requirement** | **Indicators** |
| 3.1 | The cleaning services shall include the cleaning of wards, clinics, and other areas in the hospital, such as lobbies, railings, corridors, staircases, toilets, etc., and specialized cleansing such as for operating theatres, laboratories, pharmacies, and allied areas. | The cleansing services to be provided shall be carried out in accord with good practices and shall follow the existing and developed procedures in hospitals as set out in the master agreed procedures for cleansing and the relevant MOH guidelines, as follows: | Performance indicators include the following:<br><br>a) Free from bad odours and appropriately deodorized<br>b) No surface stains<br>c) No litter<br>d) No dust<br>e) Low bacterial count. |
| 3.2 | The cleaning services shall also include cleansing of common areas where the space within the hospital compound is rented out to private vendors by the hospital administration, such as for shops, banks, post offices, etc. | a) Guidelines on the control of hospital-acquired infections by the Medical Services Division of the MOH<br>b) Disinfection and sterilization policy and practices of MOH, Malaysia<br>c) Code of practice or prevention of infection and accidents in the hospital, laboratory, and post-mortem rooms – MOH<br>d) Universal infection control precautions – MOH | Limits are as follows:<br><br>General and general area: surface count should be < 2+ on agar plate.<br><br>Operating theatres and labour rooms: surface count should be less than 1,000 per square metre using the agar impression method.<br><br>Standard microbiological air count should be < 200 CFU per cubic metre for operating theatres and < 10 CFU per cubic metre for transplant, cardiovascular, and orthopaedic surgery areas. |
| 3.3 | The cleaning services shall also include cleansing of the hospital kitchen, including its food preparation areas, except for cooking utensils. As for canteens, the public area is included except for tables and the food preparation area. | | |

| 3.4 | The cleaning services shall also include cleansing of all common areas in the hospital's training school and hostels (such as for nurses, medical assistants, etc.) and housemen's (doctors') quarters. | | f) Compliance with MOH guidelines<br><br>Each validated complaint of failing to achieve items *a*, *b*, *c*, and *e*, above, is a very serious non-conformance to service standard infraction.<br><br>For item *d*, it is a serious non-conformance to service standard infraction. |
|---|---|---|---|
| 3.5 | The method, procedures, tools, and equipment to be used for cleansing services shall be such as to meet the required standard of hygiene without causing any nuisance or interfering with the normal functioning of the areas concerned, notwithstanding the normal operating function of the cleaning equipment and processes. | Methodology of cleansing services:<br><br>a) Method which introduces dust particles to be airborne shall *not* be used. Hence, conventional sweeping using brooms shall be limited to five-foot paths in the building.<br>b) Used dry and wet mops, etc., from cleansing trolley shall be cleaned and disinfected. Equipment such as buckets, cleansing trolleys, wet and dry mop holders, handles, brushes, etc., should also be washed and disinfected.<br>c) In isolation wards (e.g. paediatric), cleaning equipment used shall be dedicated to each cubicle in the ward. | All cleansing done shall follow the approved procedures as outlined in the master agreed procedures. Any validated complaint of work not done satisfactorily shall constitute a serious non-conformance to service standard infraction.<br><br>If mixing of equipment used is detected, it shall constitute a very serious non-conformance to service standard infraction.<br><br>Each episode of using a chemical not approved by MOH shall constitute a very serious non-conformance to service standard infraction.<br><br>Each validated complaint of not following the schedule and frequency is a serious non-conformance of service standard infraction. |

| | | | |
|---|---|---|---|
| | | d) Cleaning requirements must be determined by stating the methods to be employed, using chemicals approved by MOH. These chemicals (properties) shall also be approved by the British Standard, the American Standard, the Australian Standard, or any standard recognized by MOH.<br>e) All cleaning equipment and accessories used shall be approved by MOH.<br>f) Building finishes are to be preserved with care by using the right chemicals, material, and methods, as approved by MOH. The concession company shall exhaust all possible methods of cleaning bad or stubborn stains on floors and walls to the satisfaction of MOH.<br>f) The cleansing schedule and frequency for cleaning designated areas shall be mutually agreed upon.<br>g) The CC shall supply all necessary tools, equipment, and chemicals. | |

| 3.6 | The CC shall install paper towel holders and liquid soap containers. The CC shall also supply adequate paper towels, toilet paper rolls, liquid soap, and deodorizers for all toilet facilities, washing areas, and hand-washing areas/facilities in wards, clinics, kitchen, canteens, and other specified areas in the hospitals. All installation charges shall be borne by the CC. | a) In public toilets, paper towels shall be used (hand dryers are not allowed). b) In other toilets (staff, etc.) paper hand/roll towels shall be used. c) In specialized areas, sensor-type (no-contact) liquid soap dispensers shall be used. | Adequate provisions (paper hand/toilet towels/rolls, liquid or soap dispensers, etc.) shall be supplied. Each validated complaint of failure to supply adequate provisions is a serious non-conformance to service standard infraction. |
| --- | --- | --- | --- |
| 3.7 | The services shall also include the collection from the point of generation and the transportation of general (non-clinical) waste from the areas serviced to the central storage facility for such waste in each hospital. | a) The CC shall provide bag holders on-site and collection devices for the purpose of collecting and transporting the waste from the source of generation to the central store. b) All collectors shall be available to respond once a request is made to dispose of bag holders which are already full at any one time. A response time of ten minutes (maximum) is expected once a request is made. | On-time collection following a collection route shall be assessed. Each validated complaint about late collection or deviation from the approved route shall constitute a non-conformance to service standard infraction. Each validated complaint about a late response shall constitute a non-conformance to service standard infraction. |

| 3.8 | The CC shall collect all general (non-clinical) waste in a manner which will not interfere with the normal functioning of the areas concerned nor cause any nuisance to the user. | a) The CC shall collect all general (non-clinical) waste on a daily basis or as frequently as the situation demands. The routing and timing of the collection shall be such that it will not interfere with the normal functioning of the areas concerned and approved by MOH.<br>b) General (non-clinical) waste shall not be collected with other scheduled or clinical waste. | On-time collection following the collection route shall be assessed. Each validated complaint about late collection or deviation from the approved route shall constitute a non-conformance to service standard infraction.<br><br>There shall be no mixing of waste. Each episode of mixing of clinical and general waste detected shall constitute a very non-conformance of service standard infraction. |
| --- | --- | --- | --- |
| 3.9 | The CC shall supply, in adequate numbers, black bags which shall conform to the relevant standards for the collection of general (non-clinical) waste. | a) Supply of black bags to meet one week's demand at site.<br>b) Bags shall be of adequate strength to prevent breakage under normal use.<br>c) Bags shall meet requirements in BS 6642:1985.<br>d) In the event of emergencies, the CC shall be able to immediately provide an adequate supply of bags and bag holders on time at locations specified by the director of the establishment. | Adequate supply shall be assessed based on the number of validated complaints of inadequate supply. Each validated complaint shall constitute a non-conformance to service standard infraction.<br><br>Failure of any compliance testing shall constitute a serious non-conformance to service standard infraction. |

| 3.10 | The CC shall supply containers, placing them close to the source of generation (mutually agreed designated areas) for the storage of general waste. There shall be one bin complete with lining at each permanent bed in the wards. | a) Bins shall be of required volume to meet the waste volume generated/ collected, at least for twenty-four hours. <br> b) If there is a central storage bin in a collection route, the bin should have hinged closing lids. <br> c) Bins should not be easily tipped over. When emptying the contents of the bins, the lining should be tied and disposed of. <br> d) Size, type, and usage will depend on the areas. | Adequate supply shall be assessed based on the number of validated complaints of inadequate supply. Each validated complaint shall constitute a non-conformance to service standard infraction. |
|------|------|------|------|
| 3.11 | The CC shall be responsible for the design, construction, operation, and maintenance of the central storage facility for general (non-clinical) waste, as well as supply an adequate number of suitable storage bins. | a) The design of the facility and the storage containers used shall meet the requirements of the relevant local authorities. <br> b) An existing facility shall be upgraded to meet the relevant local authority's requirements and hygiene standards. <br> c) Facility should be covered and properly ventilated. It should have cleaning and washing facilities. <br> d) All bag holders and collection devices for general and clinical waste shall be cleaned according to the frequency determined by the central store. | Failure to clean the bag holders and collection devices shall constitute a non-conformance to service standard infraction. |

| | | e) Collection of general (non-clinical) waste from the central facility for disposal shall be carried out by the local authorities. The CC shall liaise with the local authorities for continuous operation. In the absence of the local authorities, the CC shall be responsible for removal of general (non-clinical) waste daily.<br>f) After each collection, the facility should be cleansed.<br>g) All liquids/waste water from the facility shall be drained into a sewer system leading to a treatment facility. If the sewer manhole is nearby, then the CC shall connect it properly at no extra cost to the government. If the sewer manhole is far away, then the MOH will connect it.<br>h) Appropriate measures should be taken to prevent clinical or other biomedical waste from being brought to the facility. Liability is restricted to actions taken by the CC's personnel.<br>i) The facility shall be maintained such that no bad odour, insects, rodents, etc., are present. | Waste from the central store shall be collected daily. Delay in collecting the waste shall constitute a serious non-conformance of service standard infraction.<br><br>Each episode of clinical waste detected shall constitute a very serious non-conformance of service standard infraction.<br><br>Each validated complaint of a bad odour, or of the presence of insects, rodents, or other pests, shall constitute a serious non-conformance of service standard infraction. |
|---|---|---|---|

| 3.12 | The CC shall carry out joint inspections with the MOH staff on an agreed schedule in addition to holding a monthly housekeeping and performance evaluation meeting. Records of such meetings shall be made available to MOH. | All works identified shall follow the schedule and frequency of cleansing services approved.<br><br>In all emergency cases for the cleansing services, the CC shall be available to respond within the time specified, which is ten minutes (maximum), to clean spills or spots or to collect waste. | If work is not done at all, it shall constitute a very serious non-conformance to service standards infraction.<br><br>Each validated complaint about a late response shall constitute a non-conformance to service standards infraction. |
|---|---|---|---|

Notes:

- For general and medical areas, a bacterial growth rate of > 2+ on an agar is an indicator of contamination and unsatisfactory cleaning.
- A 2+ growth on an agar plate is based on the quantization of streaked plates by Barlett (1978).
- Surface bacterial counts in general operating theatres and labour rooms should be less than 1,000 per square meter, using the agar impression method.
- Under ideal conditions, a standard microbiological air count of < 200 CFU per cubic metre is permissible for operating theatres during times of non-activity. Ideal conditions include the following:

  a. Good physical layout of areas in the operating theatre
  b. Good ventilation with HEPA-filtered air and positive pressure
  c. A minimum of twenty air changes per hour
  d. Correct temperature and relative humidity

- More stringent conditions of less than 10 CFU per cubic metre are permissible for transplant, cardiovascular surgery, and orthopaedic surgery areas.

| | Linen and Laundry Services (LLS) | | |
|---|---|---|---|
| **Item** | **Scope of work** | **Requirement** | **Indicators** |
| 4.1 | The concession company shall purchase all existing laundry-related equipment (including laundry machines, trolleys, weighing machines, and boiler plant dedicated to laundry) and all existing contract hospital linen. | Costs to be determined by the Valuation Department | a) Number and frequency of each category of non-compliance with service requirements and standards<br><br>b) Quality test results |
| 4.2 | The concession company shall pay for utilities (electricity, steam, water) tapped from the contract hospital if laundry is on-site. | Rates to be determined by the government | |
| 4.3 | The concession company shall supply or provide the following:<br><br>i. New equipment/laundry plant if existing facilities are not adequate to process the required linen<br>ii. Soiled linen bags and holders/trolleys to user departments<br>iii. Additional new linens as required<br>iv. Computerized linen management information. | i. Trolleys and bags to be dedicated for linen only.<br>ii. Linen materials are to follow specifications as outlined by MOH.<br>iii. Types of linen items commonly used in the contract hospitals must be as specified.<br>iv. The MIS shall include requisition, billing, usage analysis, indication of losses, etc. | |

| 4.4 | The concession company shall supply and deliver clean linen to wards and other user departments in contract hospitals. | i. Supply and delivery is to be once a day. Time shall be as mutually agreed between the CC and respective institution. Additional delivery shall be made in case of emergency.<br><br>ii. After each delivery, the stock level in wards/departments shall be two in use for the linen store and one in use for patient-based linen. The stock level for non-patient-based linen shall be one for the linen store and one in use. For special areas such as operating theatres, delivery suites, and children's wards, stock levels are based on the rate of use. Central laundries shall have adequate stocks for emergency purposes.<br><br>iii. Supply shall be in a manner that can prevent soiling in transit and during storage. | a) Delivery of cleaned linen shall be according to agreed schedule. Each validated complaint of late delivery shall constitute a non-conformance to service standards infraction.<br><br>b) Failure to deliver linen ordered shall constitute a serious non-conformance to service standards infraction.<br><br>c) Supply of linen with dirty trolleys shall constitute a serious non-conformance to service standards infraction.<br><br>d) Storage of linen in stores which are not properly maintained shall constitute a serious non-conformance to service standards infraction.<br><br>e) Falsification of the weight of clean linen supplied shall constitute an extremely serious non-conformance to service standards infraction. |
| | | iv. Counting of cleaned linen shall be carried out at the departmental linen stores by the officer in charge of each department and the concession company's representative. | |

| | | Charges shall be according to the weight of clean linen supplied to the user department. Supply shall be authorized and verified by the officer in charge of each department. Weighing shall be verified by designated contract hospital staff. | |
|---|---|---|---|
| 4.5 | The CC shall provide a method of collection of used linen from wards and other user departments. | i. Collection shall be done daily or as required.<br>ii. Each user department shall be provided a collection trolley and bags.<br>iii. Infected linen and soiled linen shall be bagged separately to prevent cross-contamination. Infected linen shall be double bagged, one of these being an alginate-sealed or -patched bag, and washed using dedicated washing machines.<br><br>Soiled linen – White bags<br>Infected linen – Red bags (double bagged)<br>Operating theatre linen – Green bags | a) Collection of soiled linen shall be according to the agreed schedule. Each validated complaint of late collection of soiled linen shall constitute a non-conformance to service standards infraction.<br>b) Each validated complaint of soiled linen not collected within twenty-four hours shall constitute a serious non-conformance to service standards infraction.<br>c) Each validated complaint of inadequate supply of linen bags shall constitute a non-conformance to service standards infraction. |
| 4.6 | Transport of clean linen to the contract hospitals and of used linen to off-site laundries | i. Transport vehicle shall be dedicated for linen only<br>ii. Transport vehicle to be properly maintained | a) Non-compliance with the requirement shall constitute a serious non-conformance to service standards infraction. |

| 4.7 | Washing, thermal disinfection, and finishing of linen | The quality shall be according to the United Kingdom Fabric Care Research Association (FCRA) Handbook or approved equivalent standards. | a) Non-compliance with approved processes shall constitute a very serious non-conformance to service standards infraction. |
|---|---|---|---|
| 4.8 | Sampling testing of linen, chemicals, and process water | All necessary tests shall be performed as specified in the FCRA Handbook or by approved equivalent standards, including testing of whiteness, chemical residue, tensile strength, and bacteria count to ensure the quality and processes. | a) Non-compliance with the approved standards shall constitute a very serious non-conformance to service standards infraction. |
| 4.9 | Repair and replacement of linen shall be performed by CC | a) All torn linen shall be patched based on MOH linen repair criteria before delivery. b) All damaged linen shall be replaced based on MOH linen replacement criteria. | a) Non-compliance with the set criteria shall constitute a non-conformance to service standards infraction. |
| 4.10 | Training shall be provided to the contract hospital staff on matters to enhance the efficiency of service provided | | |

| Clinical Waste Management Services (CWMS) | | | |
|---|---|---|---|
| Item | Scope of work | Requirement | Indicators |
| 5.1 | The proposed services to be provided shall be for the collection, storage, transportation, treatment, and disposal of clinical waste from all the contract hospital and other MOH facilities using the clinical waste management services of the contract hospital listed in the concession agreement.<br><br>Clinical waste is defined as follows:<br><br>• Any waste which consists wholly or partly of human or animal tissue, blood, pharmaceutical products, swabs, dressings, syringes, needles or other instruments, being waste which unless rendered safe may prove hazardous to any person coming into contact with it; and | | |

| | | | |
|---|---|---|---|
| | • Any other waste arising from medical, nursing, dental, veterinary, pharmaceutical, or similar practice, investigation, treatment, care, teaching, or research, or the collection of blood for transfusion, being waste which may cause infection to any person coming into contact with it. | | |
| 5.2 | The CC shall supply, in adequate numbers, various sizes of bags and containers, including sharps containers, receptacles, and containers for on-site storage (yellow bag/light blue bag lined containers and sharps containers) to all establishments at the source of generation and locations to be specified by the director of each contract hospital.<br><br>The CC shall provide suitable containers at a central storage facility in each contract hospital. These containers shall be used to transport clinical waste from the establishment to the incinerator. | Provision of:<br><br>i. Light blue bags meeting specifications<br>ii. Yellow bags meeting specifications<br>iii. Yellow clinical containers for on-site storage, including container needed for treatment trolley meeting specifications.<br>iv. Sharps containers, including sharps containers for treatment trolley, shall meet specifications.<br>v. Stickers preprinted with the name and code of the contract hospital and serial numbers, and having a one-way plastic seal, at each point of generation are to be used to identify each yellow bag containing clinical waste and to seal such bag before collection. | All supplies must have a valid certificate issued by SIRIM or other, equivalent authority to show compliance with standards specified for this project. Failure to produce a valid certificate shall constitute a non-conformance to service standards infraction.<br><br>i. Samples of supplies shall be taken at least twice every year for compliance testing. Failure of any compliance testing shall constitute a non-conformance to service standards infraction.<br>ii. Each validated complaint of inadequate supply shall constitute a non-conformance to service standards infraction. |

| | | a) The CC shall obtain prior written approval from MOH on the design and specification of all bags and containers mentioned above before any supply can be made. <br> b) Sizes and quantity of bags and containers shall be selected to meet the requirements of the collection frequency of once every twenty-four hours from the point of generation to the central storage facility. For sources with high generation rate, a higher collection frequency can be imposed by the director of each contract hospital. The collection frequency shall be decided by the director. <br> c) An adequate supply of bags means that bags meet the relevant specification and size requirements and are available at all times at each source of generation to meet three days' need. | iii. Supplies shall be delivered to each source of generation at locations specified by the director of each contract hospital. Any validated complaint of non-delivery of supplies shall constitute a non-conformance of service standards infraction. |
|---|---|---|---|

| | | | |
|---|---|---|---|
| | | d) An adequate supply of on-site storage containers means that containers meet the relevant specification and size requirements needed by each source of generation in any contract hospital and are provided at all times.<br>e) An adequate supply of sharps containers means that sharps containers meet relevant specification and size requirements and are available at all times at each source of generation, with one in use and one as a spare.<br>f) In the event of emergency situations, the CC shall be ready to immediately provide an adequate supply of all bags, bins, and containers at locations specified by the director of the contract hospital. | |
| 5.3 | Clinical waste in yellow bags shall be collected by the CC daily, or more frequently as directed by the director of each contract hospital for sources with a high generation rate from the on-site storage to the central store. No bags or sharps containers shall be collected unless they are properly identified and secured to prevent spillage. | 1. The CC shall provide a collection trolley or wheeled bin for the purpose of collecting clinical waste from the source of generation and transporting it to the central store. The collection trolley shall meet specification in the contract. | i. On-time collection following the collection route shall be assessed. Each validated complaint about late collection or deviation from approved route shall constitute a non-conformance to service standards infraction. |

|  |  |  |  |
|---|---|---|---|
|  | Collection of clinical waste shall be carried out following an agreed time schedule and designated routes, and using a suitable collection device for such purpose. Such device shall be thoroughly cleaned after each cycle of use or when spillage has occurred. On no account shall clinical waste be collected with other waste or materials. | a) The CC shall obtain prior written approval from MOH for the specifications of the collection trolley and wheeled bin.<br><br>2. Collection of clinical waste from all sources of generation to central store by the CC:<br><br>a) Once a day unless otherwise directed by the director of each contract hospital<br>b) Timing to be decided by the director of each contract hospital | ii. Any validated complaint of non-collection of clinical waste by the CC shall constitute a non-conformance to service standards infraction.<br><br>iii. No mixing of waste. Each episode of mixing of clinical waste bags and non-clinical waste bags in a wheeled bin shall constitute a non-conformance to service standards infraction. |
| 5.4 | One cycle of use means that the collection device has completed one collection round at any one time and the load collected has been emptied before returning for the next round. | a) Routing to be decided by the director of each contract hospital.<br>b) Collection of clinical waste shall be done by using dedicated wheeled bins or a trolley, which shall be washed after each cycle of use. Such bins shall be transported to the incinerator using a dedicated truck. Following the unloading of such bins, the bins shall be washed. | i. No non-MOH waste shall be included.<br><br>Each episode of non-MOH waste detected in MOH's clinical waste stream shall constitute a non-conformance to service standards infraction.<br><br>ii. Any tag in a record sheet and in the clinical waste bag which is unsigned, or signed by an unauthorized person, shall constitute a non-conformance to service standards infraction. |

165

| | | c) All collectors shall be trained to manage spillage in accord with the emergency plan as per the procedure in the contract. All spillage-management kits are to be provided by the CC.<br>d) All collectors shall use protective equipment and clothing at all times whilst carrying out their tasks.<br>e) Provide all labour, equipment, and other related facilities for collection. | iii. Any spillage not managed according to procedure shall be considered as a non-conformance to service standards infraction.<br>iv. Any validated complaint of spillage due to negligence by the CC shall constitute a non-conformance to service standards infraction.<br>v. Any validated complaint of an untreated collection wheeled bin or trolley used for the collection of clinical waste shall constitute a non-conformance to service standards infraction. |
|---|---|---|---|
| 5.5 | The central storage for clinical waste in each contract hospital shall be a secured facility. If the collected waste is to be stored for more than twenty-four hours, refrigerated storage at 4oC to 6oC shall be provided. The central storage facilities together with all related equipment shall be provided by the CC. | **Central Storage**<br><br>a) Central stores shall be provided by the CC in each contract hospital to meet specifications. The CC shall obtain prior approval from the MOH on the design and purpose of the central store.<br>b) A central store shall be provided by the CC for each of MOH's contract hospitals at a location to be specified by the director of each contract hospital. | i. No mixing of waste is permitted.<br><br>Each episode of mixing of a clinical waste bag and a non-clinical waste bag shall constitute a non-conformance to service standards infraction.<br><br>ii. No non-MOH waste is permitted.<br><br>Each episode of non-MOH waste detected in MOH's clinical waste stream shall constitute a non-conformance to service standards infraction. |

| | | All facilities, structures, and infrastructure of the central store shall be provided by the CC up to the perimeter drain of the store. This shall include water, electricity, sewerage, and drainage facilities.<br><br>c) The storage facility shall be securely locked except during operations. The director of the MOH contract hospital and the officer authorized by the director shall be given access to the central store for inspection when demanded.<br><br>d) Weighing and documentation at the central store shall be carried out by the CC and supervised by the officer authorized by the director of each MOH contract hospital on an agreed time schedule. Records of daily waste generation and consignment dispatched shall be kept by the authorized MOH officer in each contract hospital.<br><br>e) The CC is to maintain the central store. | iii. Each case where the central store is found unlocked and at the same time unattended shall constitute a non-conformance to service standards infraction.<br><br>iv. Each case where the central store is not kept clean shall constitute a non-conformance of service standard.<br><br>v. Loss of record sheet or any tags forming part of the record sheet shall be considered a non-conformance to service standards infraction.<br><br>vi. Any validated report of falsification of weight by the CC shall constitute a non-conformance to service standards infraction. |
|---|---|---|---|

| 5.6 | For cases where a regional incinerator is used, the CC shall be responsible for the transport of clinical waste for each establishment to the final disposal facility (dedicated clinical waste incinerator). This task shall preferably be carried out on a daily basis. At the start of the contract, the CC shall supply MOH with the list of vehicles proposed for use, stating the registration numbers and load-carrying capacities by weight, volume, and number of containers. Any subsequent changes to the list shall be reported to MOH in advance. Substitute vehicles to be used in case of breakdown shall also be made known to MOH in advance. The drivers of all vehicles and any assistants to the drivers shall be properly trained to carry out the duty in a safe and professional manner and be able to manage any possible emergency situation. They shall wear appropriate protective clothing when performing their task. | **Transportation/Transfer**<br><br>a) A wheeled bin meeting specifications shall be used for the transport of clinical waste from the contract hospital to the off-site incinerator.<br>b) A dedicated vehicle meeting specifications shall be provided by the CC for the transport of clinical waste from the contract hospital to the off-site incinerator.<br>c) All such vehicles shall have a valid license to transport clinical waste.<br>d) The transport/transfer of clinical waste from the central store to the incinerator shall be carried out according to a schedule agreed by both the director and his or her authorized officer. Should there be any delay, the CC shall inform the director of the contract hospital immediately, providing information about the cause of the delay and the remedial actions been taken by the CC. | i. Waste from the central storage is to be transported/transferred to the incinerator within the specified twenty-four hours after collection. Delay without valid reason or with remedial action not accepted by MOH shall constitute a non-conformance to service standards infraction.<br>ii. Any validated stray MOH consignment or part of any MOH consignment in the custody of CC shall constitute a non-conformance to service standards infraction.<br>iii. Any case where spillage is not managed according to procedures shall constitute a non-conformance to service standards infraction.<br>iv. Using unlicensed transportation for clinical waste shall constitute a non-conformance to services standards infraction.<br>v. Any case where services provided by the CC do not meet all the pertinent legal requirements of the relevant government agencies shall constitute a non-conformance to service standards infraction. |

| | | | |
|---|---|---|---|
| | For cases where an on-site incinerator is used, the CC shall be responsible for the transfer of clinical waste from the central store to the incinerator each day. | | |
| 5.7 | The CC shall supply, install, commission, operate, and maintain dedicated clinical waste incinerators for the disposal of clinical waste with the capacity to meet the need of the MOH for the entire contract period. | **Disposal**<br><br>a) Each dedicated clinical waste incinerator must have a valid license issued by DOE. Other plants or facilities within the incineration plant which require license from the appropriate authorities for their operations must possess a valid license.<br>b) The CC shall obtain prior written approval from the MOH on the design and construction of the clinical waste incinerator.<br>c) The design, installation, commissioning, operation, and maintenance of all dedicated clinical waste incinerators, including the disposal of fly ash and bottom ash, shall meet all legal and administrative requirements of the following agencies:<br><br>i. Department of Environment (DOE)<br>ii. Local authorities | i. Any cases of illegal disposal of clinical waste consignment received and ashes produced at the incineration plant by the CC shall constitute a non-conformance to service standards infraction.<br>ii. Providing false information by CC to MOH on any matter related to clinical waste management services rendered by the CC shall constitute a non-conformance to service standards infraction.<br>iii. Any case of the consignment note not returning to MOH upon receipt of the consignment at the disposal facility shall constitute a serious non-conformance to service standards infraction. |

|  |  | iii. Factory and Machinery Department<br>iv. Other relevant agencies<br><br>d) An operating record of the incineration process shall be kept by the CC for all incinerators. For an incinerator having a capacity exceeding one ton per day, automatic recording of incinerator operations shall be provided. All operating records for the project shall be accessible by MOH through the MIS.<br>e) The CC is required to carry out all compliance testing for the emissions standard as well as other tests imposed by DOE. The CC shall also carry out all other activities to comply with requirements stipulated by other government agencies.<br>f) The CC is required to build, operate, and maintain all facilities within the incinerator plant.<br>g) The CC is required to buy existing incinerators and allied equipment from MOH, with the price(s) to be determined by the Government Valuation Department. |  |
|---|---|---|---|

# Glossary of Acronyms

| | |
|---|---|
| ACG | Automatic complaint generation |
| BAS | Building automation system |
| BEMS | Biomedical engineering maintenance system |
| BOMBA | *Fire authority in Malaysia* |
| CA | Concession Agreement |
| CAR | Corrective action report |
| CC | Concession Company |
| CCU | Coronary Care Unit |
| CFS | Customer feedback survey |
| CLS | Cleansing services |
| CLIN | Clean linen issue note |
| CM | Corrective maintenance |
| CMIS | Centralized management information system |
| COO | Chief operating officer |
| CSSD | Central Sterile Supply Department |
| CW | Clinical waste |
| CWMS | Clinical waste management services |
| CWRS | Clinical waste requisition sheet |
| DAR | Deduction assessment report |
| DCA | Daily cleaning activity |
| DF | Deduction formula |
| DOE | Department of Environment |
| DOSH | Department of Safety and Health |
| DP | Demerit point |
| DVO | Deduction valuation officer |
| ECRI | Emergency Care Research Institute |

| | |
|---|---|
| EPF | Employyees Provident Fund |
| FCRA | Fabric Care Research Association |
| FEMS | Facility engineering maintenance service |
| GF | Gearing factor |
| GR | Gearing ratio |
| HD | Hospital director |
| HEPA | High-efficiency particulate air |
| HEPPM | Hospital engineering planned preventive maintenance |
| HMR | Hospital monthly report |
| HSIP | Hospital-specific implementation plan |
| HSS | Hospital support services |
| ICU | Intensive-care unit |
| ID | Identity |
| IFMA | International Facility Management Association |
| IKRAM | *A non-governmental organization by the name of "Kumpulan Ikram Sdn Bhd"* |
| JBEG | Jabatan Bekalan Electrik dan Gas (*Department of Electricity and Gas*) |
| JI | Joint inspection |
| JKR | Jabatan Kerja Raya (*Public Works Department*) |
| JKKP | Jabatan Keselamatan dan Kesihatan (*Department of Safety and Health*) |
| KPI | Key performance index |
| KRA | Key result area |
| LLS | Laundry linen services |
| LPG | Liquefied petroleum gas |
| MA | Medical Assistant |
| MAP | Master agreed procedure |
| MDF | Main distribution frame |
| MF | Monthly fee |
| M&E | Mechanical and Electrical |
| MIS | Management information system |
| MOH | Ministry of Health |

| NCR | Non-conformance report |
|---|---|
| O&M | Operation and maintenance |
| OSHA | Occupational Safety and Health Act |
| OT | Operation theatre |
| POG | Project operations guideline |
| POP | Project operations procedure |
| PPM | Planned preventive maintenance |
| PTM | Project technical manager |
| Puspakom | Pusat pemeriksaan kenderaan berkomputer (*Computerized center for vehicular inspection*) |
| QA | Quality assurance |
| QAP | Quality assurance programme |
| QC | Quality control |
| QMS | Quality management system |
| RF | Recurrence factor |
| RI | Routine inspection |
| RTD | Road Transport Department |
| SCA | SIHAT concession agreement |
| SCM | Scheduled corrective maintenance |
| SDF | Sub-distribution frame |
| SIHAT | Sistem Hospital Awasan Taraf (*A private company*) |
| SIQ | Shortfall in quality |
| SIRIM | Standards and Industrial Research Institute of Malaysia |
| SOCSO | Social security organization |
| SPAN | Suruhan Perkhidmatan Air Negara (*National Water Services Commission*) |
| T&C | Testing and commissioning |
| TRPI | Technical requirement performance indicator |
| UM | Unscheduled maintenance |
| VVF | Variation Verification form |
| VWC | Verification of works completion |

# Sources

Act 586, Private Healthcare Facilities and Services Act and Regulations. 2006.

Concession Agreement between the Government of Malaysia and the Concession Companies. Oct 1996

"Facility Management." *Wikipedia* [website] <https://en.wikipedia.org/wiki/Facility_management> accessed 18 April 2016.

Institution of Engineers, Malaysia. *Healthcare Facility Management Reality and Challenges.* December 2013.

Jurutera, Institution of Engineers, Malaysia. *Facilities Management in Malaysia.* May 2009.

Ministry of Health, Malaysia. *QAP Manual.*

Ministry of Health, Malaysia. *Guidelines on Facility Engineering Planned Maintenance.*

Ministry of Health, Malaysia. *Guidelines for the Application of Deduction Formula for Privatization of Hospital Support Services.*

Ministry of Health, Malaysia. *User Manual for Central Integrated Nationwide Management Information System (CMIS) Version 2,* 2002.

Piper, James E. *Handbook of Facility Assessment.* New York: Marcel Dekker, Inc., 2004.

Supervisory and Consultancy Agreement between the government of Malaysia and *Sistem Hospital Awasan Taraf Sdn Bhd* (SIHAT). 1 March 2006.

Supplementary Agreement between the Government of Malaysia and the Concession Companies. 29 January 2003.